FIRE

The Earth series traces the historical significance and cultural history of natural phenomena. Written by experts who are passionate about their subject, titles in the series bring together science, art, literature, mythology, religion and popular culture, exploring and explaining the planet we inhabit in new and exciting ways.

Series editor: Daniel Allen

Fire

Stephen J. Pyne

REAKTION BOOKS

To Sonja, who saw it go from wild fire to hearth fire to quintessence

Published by
Reaktion Books Ltd
33 Great Sutton Street
London EC1V 0DX, UK
www.reaktionbooks.co.uk

First published 2012

Printed and bound in China

British Library Cataloguing in Publication Data
Pyne, Stephen J., 1949-
   Fire : nature and culture. – (The Earth)
   1. Fire – History. 2. Fire – Social aspects. 3. Fire ecology.
   I. Title II. Series
   304.2-DC23

ISBN 978 1 78023 046 7

CONTENTS

Fire, the shape-shifter.

Prologue: Three Fires

The tree – the carcass that remains of it - lies within the Desierto de los Leones National Park in the Valley of Mexico. A large gash runs down the bole where lightning once split off a long splinter. The outside of the trunk is chunky with the black, deep etchings of a subsequent fire. Later, the tree died, it is believed, from ozone and other noxious gases in the poisonous atmosphere of the valley. Then it fell, and its scars now serve as a record for historical forensics while its composite of gouges, gnarly burns and sickened physiology speaks perhaps as an oracle.

What that fallen trunk reveals will vary with the eyes that look upon it. But for anyone curious about fire, that single tableau is a rude chronicle of earthly combustion. Usefully, that story has three parts – the combustion community tends to think in terms of fire triangles in the same way the hydrological community thinks in terms of water cycles. One part of that fire story belongs to nature alone, the second to people working with nature, and the third to a Promethean humanity inventing a new kind of fire.

The first phase began in the early Paleozoic. Here, the first of fire's triangles appeared as heat, fuel and oxygen alloyed to allow combustion outside cells. As plants spread across the land another organizing triangle crystallized, this one made of terrain, weather and coarser arrays of hydrocarbon fuels, that governed how the zone of combustion moved around the landscape. For over 420 million years the overwhelming source of ignition was lightning, as bolts blasted away at plants like the gouged conifer in the Desierto, some fraction of which kindled into flame.

Then, within the last two million years, the genus *Homo* acquired the capacity to preserve and eventually start fires. In the original triangle life created two sides – fuel and oxygen – but had to yield to a physical process, the act of kindling. Now, the living world could claim all three sides, shrinking the relative impact of lightning, and not only did a species begin replacing atmospheric electricity as a source of kindling, but only one species did. *Homo sapiens* enjoys a species monopoly over fire's manipulation that it will surely never willingly allow another creature to possess.

Humans became the keystone species in fire's ecology. People commandeered fire where it naturally thrived, took it to places that had never known it, and everywhere changed the patterns through which it flourished. By setting fires – those in confined hearths and furnaces and those on the land – they remade vast

Burned tree trunk, Desierto de los Leones, Mexico.

landscapes and rendered others habitable. The charring around the Desierto trunk is most likely the outcome of just such burning. This – anthropogenic fire – is the second side of fire's historical triangle.

The last phase is more recent, perhaps no older than two centuries. It is the era of industrial fire, defined simply by the combustion of fossil biomass. This is an artificial burning: it occurs in special chambers without the biotic checks and balances of season and place. The ancient power of fire to transmute makes a modern technological leap into pipes and wires. People burn fuels from the geologic past and release their effluents into a geologic future. The present they overload with noxious emissions and greenhouse gases. The famously polluted air in the Valley of Mexico – the product of industrial combustion – is the likely cause of death for the fallen Desierto conifer. Certainly the groves around it are pale and feeble from cloying ozone and deposited acids.

The Desierto conifer is a cameo of earth's fire history. Until recently, there was little strange or unseemly about that saga. There is nothing alien about fire: the living world runs on combustion and has co-evolved with the open flame. Here is the true wildfire, the fire that can thrive quite apart from any human. It has its own logic and coded behaviour, however flamboyant it appears to untutored eyes. So too there is nothing peculiar about humanity using fire: it has been a species possession – a defining trait – since our origins. It defines our ecological agency and has gone on for so long in so many places that the prevailing regimen of fire, to which the ecosystem has adapted, is the one guided by people. This fire, too, has its prescriptions and codes. Fire is what we do that no other species does.

Industrial combustion is different, however, for it depends wholly on humanity; so powerful has the role of people become that observers have proposed that the era of fossil fuel burning constitutes a distinct geologic epoch, the Anthropocene, for which fire is not simply an index of global change but the primary driver of it. What makes the story especially fascinating is that the three fires do not simply evolve one after the other, but compete. They can all converge at the same time and place. They can all leave their imprint on the same single plant.

Nordic legends represented the living world as a colossal tree, the Yggdrasil, at the foot of which three Norns spin, weave and cut the threads that compose the tapestry of life. The Desierto conifer might serve as a symbolic Yggdrasil of fire at the base of which fuel, spark and oxygen braid together to keep the planet alive and craft its designs, for fire is truly a creation of life, without which all would turn dead and cold.

PART ONE

Fire Wild

The power of fire, or *Flame* ... we designate by some trivial chemical name, thereby hiding from ourselves the essential character of wonder that dwells in it as in all things ... What is *Flame*?

Thomas Carlyle, *On Heroes, Hero-worship, and the Heroic in History* (1841)

Albert Bierstadt, *The Conflagration*, oil on paper.

1 Creating Combustion

What we call fire is a chemical reaction, which makes it a shape-shifter; that is to say, it takes its character from its context. Alone among the classical elements, it is not a substance and has no distinctive academic discipline to claim as its own. Fire is what its environment makes it.

Unlike water, earth and air, it has no weight, cannot exist unchanged minute by minute, cannot be transported by itself and cannot be pumped or dumped elsewhere. You don't carry fire as you can air, water or earth: you carry the stuff that makes its reaction possible. Change fire's setting and you change fire's expression. This can happen within a single event, as a fire smoulders through organic soil, flares into dried grass and shrub, and flashes through the canopies of conifers. One fire, many forms.

Similarly, we rarely study fire for itself; rather, we understand fire within the context of other disciplines. Its oxidation reaction is examined in chemistry. Its heating mechanisms belong to physics or mechanical engineering. Its buoyant smoke and plumes rise out of meteorology. Its ecological effects descend from biology. Closed combustion belongs in engineering; open burning, in forestry. The only fire department in a university is the one that sends emergency vehicles when an alarm sounds. Our definition of fire thus depends on where we site the subject. In one context it is chemistry, in another physics, in still another biology, or even anthropology. We know it when we see it, but how we see it shapes how we define what we think we know.

For some 200 years the prevailing conception has situated fire within chemistry. Webster's ninth *Collegiate Dictionary* defines it as 'the phenomenon of combustion manifested in light, flame, and heat'. 'Combustion' is, in turn, defined as the act of burning, or 'a chemical process [as an oxidation] accompanied by the evolution of light and heat'. Fire results when oxygen combines rapidly with hydrocarbons, a reaction that requires some input of energy – a spark, a spasm of heat – to begin the process, and it gives off (or 'evolves') heat, light and various chemicals. It thus fits tidily into a wide spectrum of oxidation reactions. Oxidize iron slowly and you get rust. Oxidize wood rapidly and you get fire.

Thinking about fire in this way has quickened scientific research because it isolates only a few properties out of fire's milieu for investigation. This reductionism makes it possible to create gadgets based on those properties: the pyrotechnologies that underwrite much of humanity's power. In the end those devices may transcend flame altogether, or abolish fire in favour of a tightly crafted combustion, or eventually abandon burning in all forms. But while thinking about fire in this way can boost technological spin-offs – it can design better candles and build a better propane barbecue – it also makes imagining fire in its natural settings, in which it is not an isolated event but a synthesizer of its surroundings, more difficult. Those settings are profoundly biological.

The fact is, fire is not a stray chemical reaction free-floating around the planet that occasionally erupts into soaring flames. It is a process integrally embedded into life on earth. Life created fire, life sustains fire, and life has progressively absorbed fire within its ecological webs. A molecular reaction fire certainly is, but its originating chemistry is a *bio*-chemistry. Fire takes apart what photosynthesis puts together; it performs this task within a biological matrix; it has evolved hand in glove with the living world. When oxidation occurs within a cell, it's called respiration; when it occurs in the wider world, it's called fire. Stopping respiration will kill an organism; removing fire from landscapes can disrupt biota as much as shutting down sunshine or shifting the seasonality of rainfall would.

The primordial earth did not have fire: it acquired it over long aeons. Marine life in the oceans filled the atmosphere with oxygen as a by-product. Then when plants began colonizing land, they put combustible hydrocarbons into an atmosphere marinated in free oxygen and were thus readied to combust. In this way life supplied two of the sides to fire's most elemental triangle. What life could not supply (and hence control) was ignition. Instead it relied on heat sources such as volcanoes and above all, lightning.

This made fire a border-hopper between the purely physical and the purely biological. It was birthed and raised by earthly life, but was not itself alive. It responded to prompts of spark, wind and terrain, but could not subsist upon purely physical considerations. Unlike floods, typhoons and earthquakes, which can occur without a particle of life present, fire is a biophysical perturbation that cannot exist outside a biota. Although modern technology has abstracted fire from this organic context, fire did not originate as a rogue reaction and then become absorbed into the biosphere. It began as an integral feature of early life, the source of cellular power, and has since evolved with life overall. When people speak of fire gulping oxygen and feeding, it is a mixed metaphor for a reaction that is a product of life but not itself living.

In this way two forms of combustion co-emerged, which we might term 'slow' and 'fast'. Slow combustion – respiration – involves the breakdown of photosynthesized matter within mitochondria. It takes in oxygen and hydrocarbons and gives off water, carbon dioxide and energy. This process, the Krebs cycle, is tightly choreographed on a molecular level and restricted to the cellular combustion chamber. It is a physical reaction, of course, but one encased within a biological setting, joining oxygen and fuel and catalysing their splitting and fusing. The reaction cannot propagate beyond this.

But when oxygen saturates the atmosphere and hydrocarbon fuels encrust the land's surface, they can and will interact when conditions are right. The outcome – fast combustion – is what we know colloquially as fire. It burns without the rigid

constraints that a cell provides. Ignition happens on the outside. Clumps of biomass may or may not burn depending on whether they are wet with spring flush or recent rains, whether they consist of tiny, fast-reacting particles or giant, sluggish trunks with small surface-to-volume ratios, and whether the clumps are close enough that a flame can leap from one to another. Fire's spread depends on the winds and on the ability of the air mass to rise readily. Its physical confinement varies with the terrain, all but unconstrained on rolling steppes or shaped immovably by mountain valleys. Because it is not physically confined, fire is said to be free-burning as it responds to the ceaseless vagaries of its context: to the puffs and calms of wind; to bunchings of leaves and needles, grasses and scrub; to the slopes and saddles of ridges and ravines. Unlike cellular combustion, the zone of combustion moves about the landscape itself.

So, once again, fire's behaviour lies on a murky border between the physical and the biological. Life supplies the raw oxygen and the biomass, and the matrix of living (and dead) plants integrates the reaction; but wind, atmospheric stability, solar heat, gradients, ravines, mesas and the physical geographies of a site, both tiny and huge, shape the zone of combustion as it lofts upward, rushes over hillsides, slows against gusts, smoulders in peat or flashes through baked grasslands. Moreover, life does not

Fire and life: two competing combustions. William Jacob Hayes, *Prairie Fire and Buffalo Stampede*, 1869, oil on canvas.

control the source of ignition. The sides of fire's triangle evolved separately, only becoming linked when fire synthesized them in a spasm of heat.

The nature of life based on photosynthesis assures this will happen: fire will occur unless something blocks it. Everything that affects the evolution and ecology of life will thus shape fires. Yet a profound interdependence emerges out of all this, for even as life creates the conditions for fire, fire reshapes the living world. It selects for evolutionary fitness; it powers and cycles ecosystems. Fire can create conditions that promote more fire, or less. Much as its heat begins the process by which it spreads, so its history influences the conditions that allow it to propagate through time. Only one aspect remained outside life's control, ignition. But eventually that too would come within its realm, and the hybrid character of free-burning fire would nudge further from the physical to the biological.

As fire and life accommodated one another, their interactions assumed recognizable patterns – what has come to be called a fire regime. Fire, however, is not like a migratory species that returns seasonally to a place: it is constantly recreated at and by that place. It is more like a storm; and just as a given place may experience many kinds of storms and yet be different from another place, so it is with fire. A fire is to a regime as a storm is to a climate. Regimes and climates are thus statistical composites; useful, understandable and unstable. The real payoff from the regime concept is that it sharpens our appreciation of fire's biological role. One often hears the statement that such-and-such a plant is adapted to fire; this has little more meaning than the statement that such-and-such a plant is adapted to water. An organism isn't adapted to water but to a pattern of rainfall or flooding, of wetting and drying. A tree that thrives amid precipitation that falls equitably month after month will no longer be adapted if a similar amount of annual rainfall comes only during a three-month season. So it is with fire. It is not fire's presence or absence but the patterns of burning that matter. An organism is adapted not to fire but to a fire regime. Change that regime and fires may harm rather than help. Fire's removal in places that have long known it may be as ecologically damaging as its introduction to places to which it is alien.

Such distinctions can get lost in hysteria over species that are said either to be 'destroyed' by fire or to 'need' it. As Paracelsus long ago observed, a poison depends on its dosage. Too much sun or too little or too oddly distributed – any can do harm. So it is with water. And so, too, with fire.

Such has been the dominion and the grand saga of fire on earth. For over 420 million years slow and fast combustion have interacted to stash combustibles on the planet and burn them up. In places and times the two combustions could openly compete; what organisms decomposed was thus not available to burn openly. Rainforests, for example, did not burn because there was typically nothing on the floor to combust, since biological agents had already swept the surface clean; and grasslands cropped by grazers might leave little more than a fuzzy stubble for flames to creep among. But it is equally true that where biological decay was feeble, as in more arid climes, fire could flourish, and by routinely burning it could select for and against species that could thrive amid the flames. Rhythms of burning followed the rhythms of wetting and drying that grew fuels and then left them in a condition to burn.

And then, in the blink of a geologic eye, two related events upended the stately rhythms and unfolding of this narrative. The first was the arrival of a species with the capacity to start fire and thus allow life to claim the last of the triangle's sides. With the appearance of fire-wielding hominins the living world could begin wresting ignition away from lightning's lottery. *Homo* could complete the cycle of fire for the circle of life. A unique fire planet finally evolved a unique fiery creature.

The hominins quickened the tempo of fire's evolution, eventually inventing a mechanical equivalent to the Krebs cycle by which they could encase fire in ways that allowed it to 'burn' without the prospect of its propagating through built landscapes. As with the previous arrangement, fire and fuel were yin and yang. The ambition to contain fire demanded fuels that were not strewn across countryside, while abundant fuels – say, in the form of coal from the Palaeozoic – could not burn unless they had special chambers designed for the purpose. In keeping with our triangular metaphors, a third fire came into being that began to compete with the others. This one could exist only through constant tending by people.

What's in a name? Defining a phenomenon might seem arbitrary. Whether one emphasizes fire's physical or its biological traits hardly affects what it is and does, however much people stutter and scramble. But in truth it does matter, and not simply as a matter of intellectual housekeeping. How earth's keystone species for fire thinks about fire will affect what it does with fire, which has the potential to rewire the planet's combustion circuits. Which is what has happened.

We're talking now about fire in the vernacular sense: the flaming and smouldering that occurs openly on landscapes. Even so, fire is so much a creature of context that the range of perspectives by which one might view it is unbounded. Three are most relevant (we're back to triangles). One perspective dominates, one is beginning to shove against it for attention, and one, although the most powerful, remains suspect and invisible. The dominant first is a physical paradigm for fire. The emergent second is a biological model. The suppressed third is a cultural conception. Remarkably, each by itself is capable of explaining the full panorama of fire on earth, much as non-Euclidean geometries can be consistent and complete.

The physical paradigm holds that fire is a chemical reaction, the oxidation of hydrocarbons, organized by its physical surroundings. Because it identifies how to subject open combustion to controlled experiments, and how to make appliances by which to contain and apply it, this has become the prevailing conception, and it has been extrapolated from lab to field and city. The paradigm distils combustion into a (relatively) simple problem in oxidation chemistry, fire's behaviour into a three-dimensional chessboard of physical settings, and fire's relation to people into that of a tool. Understand a candle or blowtorch and you understand – allowing for environmental complexities – what fire is, what it will do, and how to control it.

The physical model says that the everyday living landscape we see is, in reality, a fire shed, an array of fuels bathed in an oxygenated atmosphere amid which fires will probe and propel themselves according to the tilts of slope, the strength of shifting winds and the abutting thickness of fuels. The physical model shapes an understanding of fire's ecology that envisions fire as a mechanical process that slams into and pours through biota, to which they must adapt as they would to storms. Addressing people more directly, it says that controlled fire is an implement or appliance, whether set in a factory or a forest. And it recommends that the proper way to control the physical chemistry of free-burning fire is through physical countermeasures such as dousing it with water or spraying chemical retardants and removing blocks of potential combustibles. What people cannot pick up and use, they must flee from. Confronted with a conflagration, people should evacuate as they would before a tsunami or flood.

Slowly emerging, however, is an alternative conception that emphasizes fire's biological character. It says that fire is, in its fundamentals, a product of life, that its reactions belong with

Glowing combustion: smouldering on the surface.

Converting Florida grass, palmetto and pine into flame.

organic chemistry and that its primary setting is biotic. Combustion feeds on biomass; fire behaves within a matrix primarily integrated by ecological factors and tested by long aeons of give-and-take evolution. Fire's defining setting is a pyric habitat organized by biological processes.

Such a perspective leads to a different relationship with fire. As a tool it resembles a biotechnology or a species of domestication, more akin to a sheepdog than to a furnace. As a problem it resembles an emergent plague more aptly than it does an earthquake, such that damaging fires are the outcome of broken biota no longer able to check and absorb a sudden contagion of combustion. Effective containment comes through ecological design. Ideally, humans can exercise more direct countermeasures through biological control or ecological engineering. Restoring or removing fire can be like reinstating or exterminating a species. Alternative analogies suggest other possible strategies beyond only fighting or fleeing. If, for example, megafires are likened to emergent plagues, then society might respond to them as it would to threats in public health, and that would not be with the equivalent of guns and planes.

And then there is that paradigm which is both the most critical and the least recognized. A cultural conception repositions fire within a social setting – literally a *landscape*, a land shaped by the minds and hands of humanity. The reason we study fire, the ambitions we have to boost its good side and quash its bad, the extent to which its absences and eruptions are seen as problems – all reside in its relationship to people. Fire's fundamentals, that is, are found in ideas and institutions. They reflect values and beliefs and the social mechanisms to resolve them. Even the need to choose among the intellectual models of fire – whether to prefer a physical model over a biological, for example – reside in society.

Fire's cultural environment: Eero Jarnefeldt, *The Wage Slaves*, 1893, oil on canvas. Apart from its details – the special clothing, the tools – the painting speaks to social economics, for the pictured swiddeners have become a class of migrant labourers who do the work for absentee landowners.

In this conception the critical dynamics are those that govern how people understand the world around them and act on those understandings. Fire problems are thus cultural in nature: they represent breakdowns in how people live on the land. Large unwanted fires – 'unwanted' being itself a social judgment – more resemble episodes of social unrest such as riots or insurrections than purely natural events. They can be best answered by cultural countermeasures; by reforms in policy, by better research or education, by sharper execution in agencies dedicated to fire management. What fire integrates is a social setting.

For earth's originating fires the cultural model is irrelevant since there were no humans around to witness, fuel, kindle, denounce, douse or otherwise fuss over and comment upon nature's vestal flames. It's an observation worth pausing over. Humanity did not invent fire. We discovered how to capture, tame and divert to our own purposes a process that has existed since the early Devonian. Even granting a very generous span for hominin fire (say, to *Homo erectus*) amounts to less than half a per cent of the time fire has flourished on earth. Since that moment, however, fire and humanity have co-evolved in what looks very much like a symbiosis in which each amplifies the other.

Yet ultimately the relationship is deeply unequal. Remove fire, and humanity will soon wither away. Remove people, and fire will adapt and re-establish its own stable regime. The firepower of humanity depends on the power of wild fire; the properties of tame fire derive from its wild sire. People reshape fire and have leveraged its presence on the planet, but with or without people, fire will endure as a trait both intrinsic and unique to earth.

2 Burning Bright, Burning Wide, Burning Deep

Burning bright: combustion

If oxygen and biofuels spontaneously reacted on contact, earth would be everywhere and routinely afire, which it is not. Most potential fuels are not in a form that easily and rapidly oxidizes on their surfaces. They are solids that remain stable in an atmosphere saturated with oxygen. Some spontaneous combustion does exist, but not much (closely stacked peat slabs and freshly piled woodchips, which are exposed to oxygen and decomposition, for example, but both are the result of human acts). Instead, the process of kindling a fire requires an outside jolt, a spark or blast of heat, to start processes that break down chunky biomass into suitable forms. Much as chewing and digestive processes precede slow combustion, so chemical preparations precede fast combustion.

In reality it can be as tricky to start a fire as to stop one. Heat, fuel and oxygen – each has its own dynamic and may check and balance the others while converging at the right time and place. This holds true even for heating, which initiates the kinetics of combustion. Wood is a poor conductor (one reason cooking utensils have wooden handles). Radiation decays with the square of the distance between source and sink, which makes heating difficult on the scales involved in landscapes. Convection rises, while most fuels reside on the surface. All three processes act only on the exterior, so the mass of fuel matters less than the magnitude of its exposed surfaces. The same holds for oxygen: the reaction only occurs along the thin edging where wood and air meet. A place strewn with conifer needles, grasses and fine-branched shrubs will burn better than one stacked with giant tree trunks. (Consider the effect of tossing dry needles into a campfire rather than a round of green wood.)

The heating begins the chemical 'digestive' process by which unburnable solids become combustibles. Heat must first drive off, or distil, the free water that exists within; wet fuels are non-fuels. A fuel's moisture content is, along with its thinness, the primary predictor of its combustibility. A dry particle with 25 per cent moisture content will not burn; live particles will only burn if their oil content is so high they can combust fiercely enough to boil off the internal water. Fuel moisture is both the critical and the most changeable variable in determining whether an object is likely to burn. This holds at all scales, from the wetting and drying of a particle to the wetting and drying of landscapes. In some places, this process happens annually; in others, on a scale of decades or centuries. The rhythms of water shape the regimens of fire.

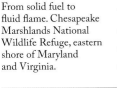

From solid fuel to fluid flame. Chesapeake Marshlands National Wildlife Refuge, eastern shore of Maryland and Virginia.

Backing fire, burning against the wind at Stillwater National Wildlife Refuge, Nevada.

With water boiled off, the heating acts on hydrocarbon solids: first, by severing chemical bonds, and second, by converting what remains into gas. This thermal cracking is known as pyrolysis, and it can guide the subsequent chain of combustion down a variety of paths. If the heating is slow, the volatile chemicals can leach away in a process not unlike the making of charcoal that leaves char and tar. If rapid and intense, it spews out gases. The solid char continues to burn by direct oxidation on its surface, while the gases burn as bubbles of flame. The solid-sited combustion is called *glowing* and the gaseous combustion *flaming*, in which bubbles, streamers and waves bear witness to fire as an expression of fluid dynamics.

Most fires in natural settings are medleys of combustion in which preheating, pyrolyzing, glowing, flaming, the as-yet-unburned or the outright unburnable are present simultaneously in different parts of the fire. Some fires, those in organic soils, rarely flame. Others, in dry grasses, may vanish in flame with hardly a hint of glowing. But most places are composites of particles big and small, scattered and continuous, relentlessly dried and wetted – sites complex and changing. They display many kinds of burning at the same time and burn variously at different times.

Burning wide: fire behaviour

Fires grow. They mature and they spread. They are born, age and die. Once grown they browse through landscapes in search of food, for wild fire does not remain where it originates. It can't, for to stay is to starve.

Every fire has its life cycle. Something has to spark it into existence; the reaction must then release more heat than it absorbs; and when the advancing front exhausts its fuels, it withers away. In nature the process happens often enough that we overlook how capricious and audacious it can be, or perhaps we recall our own ability to assemble the parts deliberately to make fire and forget that nature does not have an agent or broker to do the same. In nature's economy of fire there is no visible hand to stoke flames with new fuel and fan them with fresh oxygen, so burning is spasmodic, and even the most eruptive fires demand a set of conditions that will not long persist. They can arrive abruptly into the world, and can leave it almost as quickly.

While here, however, they move. This fact, too, is disguised by our experience with tame flame in which we fail to appreciate how a candle's flame spreads downwards into tallow, a campfire's flame sinks deeper into its larger logs, a hearth's flame spreads into the new wood stacked upon it. A Bunsen burner's flame appears to hold steady only because new gases are rising through it or, to put the matter another way, the flame is burning downwards as fast as fresh gases are rushing upwards. In landscapes the commonsense view is that fire spreads into fresh combustibles, most rapidly where those fuels are thin and easily ignited. (As

Trees torching, as a surface fire moves into the conifer canopy, Canadian boreal forest.

the old adage goes, the fine fuels drive the fire.) But it is equally possible, if a bit dizzying, to imagine the flame as constant and the landscape as passing through it.

Such a perspective would explain the abundance of shapes a flame can assume. If heat, fuel and oxygen describe the zone of combustion, another triangle of factors, roughly lumped together as terrain, weather and fuels, describes the behaviour of that combustion zone as it moves over the fire shed. Where the flaming zone meets slopes and ravines; when it encounters humidity and rushes with or against winds; as it confronts patches of grasses, brush, trees, windfall and peat – at each altered instant it burns differently, and that difference is manifest in the various shapes its propagating front assumes. The stronger the wind or steeper the slope the more a fire perimeter resembles a narrowing ellipse, morphing from something shaped like a lump of coal into the slimming geometry of a cigar. Conversely, a powerful convective column, like a magnetic torus, can hold flames within its slow-whirling ambit. Jumble terrain, winds and flora together into a single setting and it is no surprise to find that even a single fire may exhibit a suite of flames, only loosely linked.

Such fires are free-burning in that they respond 'freely' to prompts from their setting; they are not rigidly confined within a combustion chamber, fed refined fuels through a nozzle or blasted with streams of oxygen. They burn rude biomass organized by evolutionary ecology amid lithic landforms and the soft turbulence of the atmosphere. Yet their responses are neither arbitrary nor unconstrained. Terrain has borders that say where fire can and can't go. Air masses have a layering (and stability) that serve as ceilings, and borders between them that can act as barriers to movement. Biota are full of buffers and baffles, their assemblages

Chaparral fire, southern California. A good illustration of brushy, volatile fuels, topography, and a smartly developed convective column.

Steep mountains in southern California help shape a towering convective column, resulting in pyro-cumulus, *c.* 1924.

of plants richly varied as to shape, chemistry and moisture. The effects of such factors can be separately predicted, but their collective behaviour can be kaleidoscopically complex.

Fire practitioners – fire fighters and fire lighters – reduce this daunting complexity into rules of thumb that allow them to make working guesses about where a fire will go, when it will arrive and how savagely (or meekly) it will burn. Most mathematical models for fire behaviour simplify the scene into patterns of surface spreading, as wind and slope cause the flaming front to bend

A more diffuse plume resulting from the Arnica fire in Yellowstone National Park, 2009.

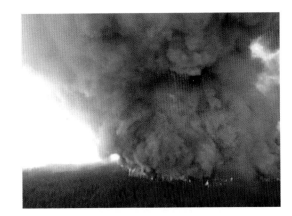

Using convection to control a prescribed burn at the Lower Klamath National Wildlife Refuge by having a strong plume draw the fire inward.

towards or away from new fuels that receive its radiated heat. Relative to the earth on which it rests and the air into which it rises, the zone of combustion appears to narrow, dwindling to the point that it can be considered flat.

But the reality is otherwise. The reality is a thick, aerodynamic swirl of fluids, as the gases released by pyrolysis mingle with or pass around those in the ambient air. Fires are atmospheric events, as much as dust devils and hurricanes, which also organize heat released on the surface. Above that flaming zone a plume emerges, which if sufficiently powerful can maintain itself such that even gusting winds can only bend, not break, it. Little wonder then that flame is such a shape-shifter. It twists and swirls as it burns along the rough border between earth and air, rising from a solid platform to flap boldly amid the free fluids of sky and fire-made gases.

Patch burns in boreal crown fires, Yakutia, Russia, 1991. The stripes of unburned trees result from the pulsed 'breathing' of the fire.

Burning deep: fire in geologic time

Each facet of fire's triangle has a history, has what in truth are very ancient chronicles that reach back to the origins of life on earth. Each has evolved separately, yet entangles and braids with the others. They came together – created fire – for the first time around 420 million years ago. They left their spoor, a kind of lithic graffiti known as fusain, in sedimentary rocks of the early Palaeozoic.

Fusain is fossil charcoal, a black carbon residue of incomplete combustion. Few natural fires burn thoroughly, particularly if the combusting particles are large. Some fragments will lose only their volatiles: that is, they will expel or shed those chemicals easily converted to gas, and when that flash of flame is gone, they cannot continue to generate the heat necessary to keep burning through the insulating material. A certain fraction, the part rich in salts or not made of hydrocarbons, will never burn, and will survive as mineral ash. So complex are most natural settings that even robust fires will burn spottily, leaving some patches untouched and others scorched or seared. All such survivors can enter the geologic record.

They are fossils of fire's evolution: they testify to earthly fire's ever-morphing shapes and abundances. Fire burned brighter

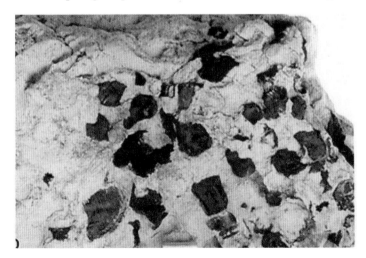

Fire in deep time: charcoal fragments embedded in Moor Grit sandstone, middle Jurassic, Yorkshire, England. Most fusain is smaller grained, a kind of silt.

during epochs when the atmosphere had higher oxygen content; it burned more rapidly when finer plants such as grasses appeared; it smouldered in near-shore peat bogs and flared amid drier conifers. Just as some places burned frequently and others rarely, so some geologic times swelled with fire and some, in effect, banked their coals. Although the chemistry behind the reaction remained unaltered, the expressed fire changed with its context. A bacteria and a Bactrian camel both rely on the Krebs cycle, but they look nothing alike, and so it is with fire. Permian fires were probably as distinct as Permian flora. The Jurassic had its pyric dinosaurs, the Cretaceous its burrowing fire-mammals. And there were moments of catastrophe and extinction. The early Mesozoic appears as an almost fire-free zone. The Cretaceous–Tertiary boundary is a fresco of charcoal.

The general chronicle of planetary fire tracks the abundance of oxygen and fuel. The earliest terrestrial plants appear in the Silurian, although they apparently did not thicken sufficiently to carry fire until the Devonian, when the first fusain appears. The atmosphere then had an estimated oxygen level around 13 per cent, compared to today's 21 per cent. The first forests, an increase in oxygen and a sharp rise in fusain followed, all of which reached a climax during the Carboniferous. There was much more to burn: this was, after all, the era that piled up coal beds as well as fusain. There was also far more oxygen, the reactive chemical, to combine with it; estimates suggest that oxygen levels rose to 35 per cent, which led to a kind of gigantism, with roaches as big as beagles, dragonflies the size of vultures and perhaps fires of comparable exaggeration. Certainly, charcoal piled up. Among Carboniferous coals fusain amounts to 10 to 20 per cent of seams.

It is not clear just what the originating fires that left such deposits looked like. More biomass does not by itself mean more burning, since only a fraction is really available as fuel and what matters most is the small particles. Nor does more oxygen mean spontaneous combustion across landscapes. The reaction can only take place on the fuel surface, and moisture content is at least as significant as oxygen content. The preserved texture of charred plants suggests fires as variegated as the landscapes in which they burned; there are fossil records for fires amid conifer forests, fern patches and mires. That fires might occur in thick organic soils is hardly unusual. Even today such places burn when drought or deliberate draining lowers their water table. Tropical peats in Southeast Asia are a major source of greenhouse gases; peat fires around Moscow in 1972 and again in 2010 smothered the city in smoke; the largest American fire of 2007 burned in the desiccated Okefenokee Swamp along the Georgia–Florida border. Even a fire but once a century could account for the thick lenses of Carboniferous charcoal.

What had leveraged up then leveraged down. Oxygen levels dropped during the Pennsylvanian and returned to their former proportions during the Triassic. Then they rose again, reaching a maximum around the time of the Cretaceous–Tertiary boundary, a period of mass extinctions and mass combustion. From that time atmospheric oxygen has dropped in a stately slide to contemporary levels. The fossil record shows similar crests and troughs, but they do not neatly align with those of oxygen. There is scant charcoal where the Palaeozoic and Mesozoic meet, but plenty in the late Mesozoic and extensive but shallow deposits throughout the Tertiary. Overall, the trend is downward, with apparently less fusain in recent epochs than in the past. The rhythms of charcoal do not map precisely with those of oxygen.

Why? The chronicle may simply reflect accidents of archiving in which epochs of widespread swampland do a better job of preserving fusain. Slow-burning soils stay put, and after being burned the site re-floods. But more dynamic explanations are likely, for oxygen is only one part of fire's triangle. The biota that modellers simplify in almost cartoonish fashion into a lumpish 'fuel' is, in reality, the outcome of a ceaselessly changing and complex evolution of biomass producers and consumers, among which fire darts like a bustling scavenger. A shift to higher proportions of lignin in plants, a change in the climate or geography of shallow seas or the emergence of a new browser (or of a carnivore that feeds on browsers) will affect the character and quantity of fuels available to burn. Laboratory experiments that manipulate

Coal seam fires, East Kalimantan, Borneo. The seams have been burning for over 11,000 years.

oxygen to combust identical samples of prepared fuels do not represent fire's true circumstances, in which open combustion must synthesize all of its surroundings, not just a single chemical.

In some respects the long chronicle is one in which fire becomes more prevalent and persistent but perhaps less eruptive or preserved. The appearance of grasses in the Miocene (and later, of C_4 grasses), for example, would have promoted more frequent fire but left much sparser records. The eras that hold the most fusain are, not surprisingly, those that have left the vastest deposits of fossil biomass generally. With regard to fire's deep history, the geologic record speaks not so much to the amount of burning as to its antiquity and breadth. The basics of fire research do not fundamentally alter until humanity arrives, fire-stick in hand, to act as a broker between fuel and flame.

It is worth emphasizing that this new factor does not represent a change in physical conditions such as climate or oxygen content. The advent of human intervention brought the third element of fire's triangle, ignition, under biological control. As an illustration of how this has rewritten the master narrative, consider the fires that plagued European Russia during the summer of 2010. The most stubborn (and unhealthy) fires burned in extensive organic soils that were drained during the Soviet era to expose peat for harvest as a fuel to feed power plants. People thus shifted combustion from the natural rhythms of drought and lightning that had governed how those mires had hitherto burned,

A fire in 2011 reburns areas of the Great Dismal Swamp National Wildlife Refuge burned in 2008. The black bear and cub are likely to be foraging in the newly opened and enriched landscape rather than despairing. Bears do not feed on old-growth forest or swamp.

to the industrial rhythms of economics and dynamos. A powerful drought and heatwave then met hundreds of human-kindled fires, and the burning peat became virtually inextinguishable. The only solution was to re-flood the swamps or wait out the season.

There is nothing new about burning peat. Cold or warm, boreal or tropical, organic soils in the form of swamps, mires and peatland have burned as far back as the Carboniferous. They have burned in more recent millennia when humans fired them either deliberately or accidentally; and they have burned again in recent decades, under a still different regimen, when people have attempted to convert them to fields, pastures and palm oil plantations. Wholesale draining and mining to export peat as fuel for electric power plants, however, is an innovation of recent years – an enterprise to strip away, relocate and redefine the very character of combustion, a kind of pyric equivalent to the attempt to create a New Soviet man. But the past is not so easily erased; the burning peats that have obscured Moscow and shut down Sheremetyevo airport are the continuation of processes that date back hundreds of millions of years; they burn deeply not only through layers of biomass but of time. Each episode sits within others, like nested dolls. Their collective story is, in miniature, the history of fire.

PART TWO

Fire Tamed

I know whence I originate! / Like a flame insatiate /
... Surely, flame is what I am.
Friedrich Nietzsche, *Ecce Homo* (1888)

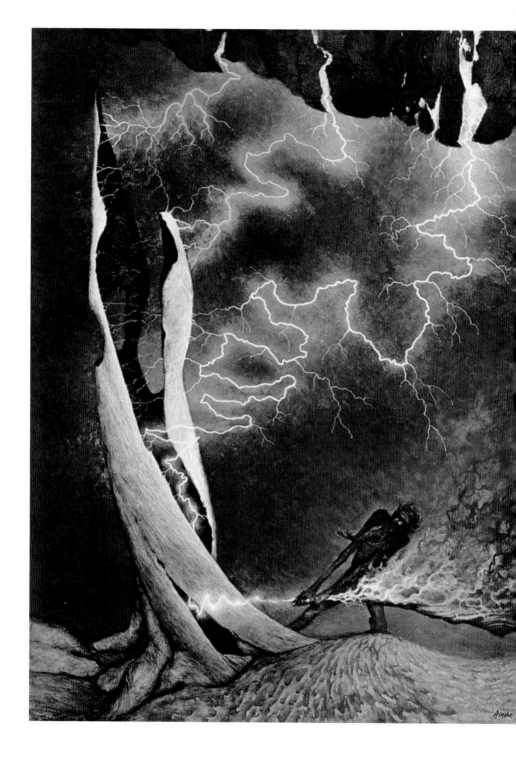

3 Fire Creature

The grand narrative of fire ebbed and flowed as climatic tides sloshed over and against the shores of evolution. Species came and went, fire regimes assembled and broke apart, fire appeared often in some places and never in others. But all such changes were variations on a theme: the basics of fire's presence remained unaltered. New combinations emerged and old ones reappeared as the biotic deck was reshuffled and new hands were dealt.

Then it changed. In the most revolutionary event since flame appeared in the Devonian, a creature acquired the capacity to manipulate fire directly. How it happened is not known. Nor is when exactly it occurred. Or in what ways the capture of fire affected landscapes beyond impermanent torches and hearths. But once started, humanity, like fire, and together, humanity and fire, propagated like a flame that would eventually burn over and remake the whole of the planet. It was the most radical event across more than 400 million years of earth's fire history.

So while the earth had long experienced fire, it had not truly known a fire creature – one that did not, as so many organisms did, adapt to fire, but rather one that exploited fire to make the world adapt to it. Yet as an enabling technology, fire made an improbable tool because it was not a thing but a reaction, and not something that acted by itself but a profoundly interactive process, an ecological fulcrum that could move whole biota. As a tool fire represented a change in kind and so did the species that wielded it. The creature that possessed fire had a power unlike any species before it.

A visual narrative of lightning being seized into an Aboriginal firestick.

Tending fire

The hominins understood tools. The patriarchal species, *Homo habilis* ('handy-man'), was named for the association of his anatomical relics with primitive stone implements. The idea of a tool was not novel, and nor was fire rare in the surroundings in which he flourished. Southern and eastern Africa was awash with natural flame. Wetting and drying determined the seasons and lightning functioned as an electrostatic match that was especially effective during the transition from dry to wet. Virtually all the flora and fauna had to cope with it to survive.

The trick for the habilines was to turn fire from a feature of their surroundings to something under their control. But while modified stone and bone could resemble arms, hands, nails – could augment humanity's feeble talons, jaws and limbs – fire was different. Surely early hominins trekked across their burned landscapes and learned to scavenge among fire's occasional kills. Fire was not something they discovered but something they seized and learned to redirect to their own purposes. At some point they would pick it up as they would have a stray stone, perhaps unintentionally, as eagles and kites do in northern Australia; and somewhere, they would grasp the unburned end of a fire-stick or scoop up embers as they might have stone flakes, and apply them to some task. The seized fire became a tool.

But its peculiar character made it a very peculiar kind of technology. It was, certainly in its origins, not made but found, and once grasped it dissolved. A stone chopper or sharpened bone could hold its form; fire could not. It had to be continually sustained or reignited. It could only be reacquired from nature seasonally, which argued for keeping it constantly alight or banked in ash. The ability to manufacture it came later, along with better technologies for striking and drilling. Sooner rather than later someone would have seen sparks cast from colliding stones or smoke flitting from abrading wood. If tinder was nearby, the toolmaker became a fire-maker. *Homo erectus* could maintain fire, but probably not until *Homo sapiens* could humanity make it. Many fire origin myths tell how fire, once stolen or sometimes given,

Patch burns: three
states of burned and
regrown prairie at
Tallgrass Prairie
Preserve, Oklahoma,
2009.

escapes into the world at large where it resides in wood, stone and grass tree until conjured out by human contrivance. Even so, aboriginal societies well into modern times, such as Australian Aborigines and Andaman Islanders, preferred to carry fire with them rather than continually start anew.

Once alit fire required constant attention. It demanded relentless foraging for fuel, endless fiddling to prevent it from burning what its holder wanted saved, and both manual skill and ambient sensitivity to ensure that it could, in fact, burn what the user wanted burned. Unlike other tools, you do not carry fire but the stuff that makes fire possible and sustains it. Such demands exceed the capacity of any single individual; only a group can care for fire and still have time left for other activities. The model for such behaviour is surely raising children, an analogy still present in many languages (in English, 'kin' and 'kindling' have the same etymological root). Before it remade landscape ecology, fire reformed social relationships.

The peculiarities multiply. You do not 'use' fire as you would a scraper or chopper, for example, but place it in circumstances where it can react as you wish. It assumes the form its context allows; fire use means shaping that context. It has the properties, that is, of the living world. Although not itself alive, it breathes

Nature's fire drive outside Darwin, Northern Territory, Australia, 1986. The flames flush out insects, mammals and lizards, which attract predators, culminating in kites and wedge-tailed eagles.

Philip King's water-colour of an Aborigine family with a firestick – the first rendition of the Australian Aborigine by a European artist. Unsurprisingly it shows them – even the child – with a fire-stick. William Blake subsequently redid the image as an engraving.

and eats; it warms, it moves, it sounds. It must be tended, bred and trained. It must be sheltered (literally, domesticated). When left, it is buried. As a tool it more closely approximates a biotechnology than a mechanical one. It behaves more like a sheepdog or dairy cow than an axe.

Mechanical tools, moreover, substitute for muscle and claws. With fire the closest analogue, however, is not to hominin anatomy but to physiology. Burning more resembles digestion than striking or scraping, which helps explain why cooking is the prototype and paradigm for pyrotechnologies generally.

Consuming fire

The first of the great changes wrought by fire were internal. They changed the creature that held the torch, who then turned that power outwards. The medium, and model, was cooking. Roasting, grilling and sautéing foodstuffs led to cooking stone, sand, metal, liquids, wood, whatever might be converted into usable forms by controlled heating. A common flame transmuted them all.

Cooking is a simple process with complex results. Heating adds value to raw biomass: it makes eating easier and more efficient and can amplify nutritional value. It converts lumps of hydrocarbons into physiological fuel. It denatures protein, gelatinizes starches and otherwise renders foodstuffs more digestible. It remakes barely edible starches into higher-caloric carbohydrates. It detoxifies foods of many harmful chemicals and kills off worms, bacteria and other disease-bearers and parasites. It leverages a given harvest of biomass, perhaps marginal, into foodstuff capable of sustaining an organism. More items can be eaten and with greater payoff. Cooked tubers have a higher caloric content than uncooked meat.[1]

So radical a change in diet encouraged a restructuring of physiology and morphology. The outcome was the most dramatic suite of anatomical changes ever recorded among the hominins. With less need to break down biomass mechanically and chemically, humans have, compared to cognate primates, a downsized mouth, stomach and intestines. We have smaller teeth and jaws since fire has already done the preliminary mastication. We have tinier stomachs and intestines since fire has begun the biochemical breakdown of fibre and meat. We no longer need a massively muscular skull or a gargantuan digestive tract. Our head can become big and our gut small. We can process ideas rather than herbage. Such reforms cannot be deduced from environmental changes alone; but once they occurred, they were encoded in our genome. We became physiologically dependent on cooking.

In recent times various food cultists have experimented with diets dedicated solely to raw fare. Since cooking, as Claude Lévi-Strauss observed in *The Raw and the Cooked* (1964), is identified with civilization, it is also bound with civilization's discontents, among them a legitimate wariness towards the excessive processing of foodstuffs that has rendered so much of modern food unhealthy. Yet Lévi-Strauss was right. Humans cannot survive on raw offerings alone, even when they have access to fresh foods year round and add nutritional supplements. People without fire cease to be people, not just symbolically but physiologically, because without cooked food they cannot find sufficient energy to survive, and thus cannot reproduce. In eerie ways experiments with raw food-only diets echo old myths about the origins of fire, which universally consider uncooked food as the most desperate of deprivations.[2]

The pyric paradigm, from hearth to habitat

Thus the process by which pyrotechnology has been able to remake the world began with humanity first remaking itself. Control over fire changed human anatomy and physiology and became encoded in our evolving genome. Equally, fire altered behaviour, since people now had to commit to its ceaseless tending, and around the fire people gathered to eat, socialize, instruct and tell stories. Not least, fire affected humanity's sense of itself. Other tools had cognates among fellow creatures, but only humanity had fire. Its possession was a Faustian bargain that self-consciously set humanity apart from all other species.

The cooking fire became the pyrotechnic paradigm for nearly all fires' uses, as hearth morphed into furnace, forge and Bunsen burner. One could cook wood to harden it into spear points or convert it to potash; cook, bake or roast stone to soften it for easier flaking; melt sand into glass; smelt ore into metals; and harden clay into ceramics. With flame one could fell and hollow out trees. With fire one could crack rock to tunnel mines. Whatever one did, fire could quicken and strengthen its fundamental reactions. It was the *organon* of alchemy, the methodology of modern chemistry, and a broad-spectrum catalyst for practically everything people did. Through fire humans made earth habitable, and through fire they have left the planet for other worlds.

Frontispiece to Book II of an edition of *The Architecture of Marcus Vitruvius Pollio*. Control of fire as measure of civilization.

Commentators of all disciplines have long appreciated that fire lies at the basis of technology, and hence of humanity's power, and is therefore a defining feature of human identity and ecological presence. In *Prometheus Bound* (attributed to Aeschylus, fifth century BC), the author has the tortured Titan, viciously punished by Zeus, proclaim that the fire he brought to a enfeebled humanity made possible 'all the arts of men', and beyond that practical purpose, fire and hope 'caused mortals to cease foreseeing doom'. In his *Natural History* (first century AD) Pliny the Elder marvelled how 'fire is necessary for almost every operation . . . It is the immeasurable, uncontrollable element, concerning which it is hard to say whether it consumes more or produces more.'[3] In his summary of Renaissance lore, *De la pirotechnia* (1540), Vannoccio Biringuccio observes that almost all technology was pyrotechnology because it depends 'on the action and virtues of fires'. In

1720, well into the scientific revolution, the physician Herman Boerhaave announced that 'if you make a mistake in your exposition of the Nature of Fire, you error will spread into all the branches of physics, and this is because, in all natural production, Fire . . . is always the chief agent.'[4] Since then, so profound has been the consequence of the shift in humanity's combustion habits from burning surface biomass to fossil fuels that it has come to define a new historical epoch, the Anthropocene. The central fire endures, even if, like the eternal flame in the Temple in Jerusalem, it remains invisible to quotidian life.

Humanity's fires no more stayed by the hearth than humanity did. They foraged, they hunted, they wandered. Instead of bringing objects to the fire, people took fire to a wider world. They used flame not just as a physiochemical reaction but a biochemical one. They burned landscapes. They began to cook the earth itself.

Modern thought, like modern science, tends to be reductionist. It imagines the simple, then builds into the complex. But the hominin experience with fire was likely the reverse. It began with the complexity and ubiquity of fire in the ambient world. Early hominins would have seen how fire worked on landscapes because that burning habitat was the world in which they lived, hunted and foraged. They would have noted, as even casual tourists to African savannahs can today, that wildlife gravitates to newly greening areas that succeed burns since such sites offer the most succulent and protein-rich grasses. They understood that fire made those landscapes palatable to grazing animals as cooking did raw meat and tubers for themselves. An extraordinary pantry of game and plants clustered on the burned patches; this was where you went to find food. Early hominins were among those fire-drawn species.

It is a commonplace that all organisms shape their habitats in ways that render them more favourable. But, until *Homo*, no creature ever had the power to restructure landscapes wholesale. It is as though African antelopes or North American bison acquired the capacity to determine when and where the greening patches on which they grazed would appear. Even beavers, famous ecological engineers, redesigning woodland watersheds, seem paltry in comparison; to achieve a comparable effect, they would have to trigger routine floods that gently or violently spread over landscapes. Burning, however, is a more protean process than watering. Fire spreads, fire interacts, fire catalyses. To control it, even if only to determine where and when to kindle and then let natural circumstances dictate the outcome, is an extraordinary capacity. With each burn, control could improve not only through acquired experience but because the landscape itself could change to better accommodate the new regime. Still, control was often tenuous since the nominally tame could go feral, and loosing fire could resemble training a grizzly bear to dance. Its firepower, however, granted humanity a biotic leverage far beyond choppers or atlatls. It allowed hominins to engineer whole ecosystems.

As with simple physical pyrotechnologies, this biological pyrotechnology expanded. It underwrote fire hunting, fire foraging, fire farming, fire herding, even fire fishing (the lights would draw fish to where they could be speared). In effect, the hominin diet was twice cooked: once in the field, and again in the hearth. Almost everything people did on the land, somewhere in its great chain of technic being, had fire. The eternal fire in humanity's temples had its analogue in the inextinguishable fires they distributed over the lands they worked. Fire-planet earth had found its keystone species.

From fire in the hand to fire in the mind

As it moved from hand to head, fire entered an ecology of folklore, myth, science and philosophy. It became a symbol of civilization and an enduring emblem of learning. It served, for centuries, as an informing principle of how the world worked and humanity's place within it. It was what moved humanity to the top of the food chain. But while it became deeply metaphoric, it did so as a source, not an object. Things behaved like fire. Fire did not behave like anything else.

Modern fire scientist in Sweden ignites test plots by using a traditional device, a patch of birch bark on a pole.

All this made sense in times when fire was prominent in quotidian life, when open flame heated and lit up houses, cooked food, forged metals and hardened pottery, refreshed pastures and readied arable fields, when the first act upon waking was to make a fire and the last act before retiring was to bank its coals. It was simple to abstract from that daily life a world in which fire performed for earth what it did for humanity's *domus*. Thus the Pre-Socratic natural philosopher and mystic Heraclitus made fire the fundamental operation and symbol for nature. What is striking is the way those flames, even if abstracted into symbols, have continued into modern times and disciplines. A recent study summarized the modern roll call of fire commentators in this way:

> Carl Sauer, a geographer, put fire close to the origins of humanity's environmental powers. It was what enabled early humanity to break 'the limitations of environment that had previously confined him' and start 'a new way of living.' Loren Eiseley, naturalist (and mystic), concluded that fire was 'the magic that opened the way for the supremacy of *Homo sapiens*' and considered humanity itself 'a flame.' Teilhard de Chardin, paleontologist (and mystic), likened the origins of thought, that is, consciousness, to a flame

'that bursts forth at a strictly localized point,' an echo, as Rachel Landau has observed, 'of the divine spark of the doctrine of special creation.' Claude Lévi-Strauss, anthropologist (and mystic of semiotics), accepted fire as the chasm between culture and creatures, parsed the world into the raw and the cooked, and declared that 'through [fire] and by means of it, the human state can be defined with all its attributes.' The British structuralist Edmund Leach then so rose into abstraction that he declared that people 'do not have to cook their food, they do so for symbolic reasons to show that they are men and not beasts.' So far had industrial humanity come from its roots and so fatuous had formal discourse about fire become.[5]

Perhaps fire had worked on the human mind as it had on the hominin gut, for it has persisted as a defining feature of culture even as it reincarnates into more modern avatars. Like Prometheus, who gradually metamorphosed from a mythological Titan into the personification of the inspired inventor, or simply of the defiant rebel, fire has itself transmuted from a creation story to a virtual presence. But not entirely. Fire yet remains at the heart of earthly ecology and for the past century a driver for global change. Its power even as a metaphor and source of inspiration seems inexhaustible. As Plutarch observed, the mind is not a vessel to be filled. It is a fire to be kindled.

4 Fire Works: Anthropogenic Fire Practices

Tending fire was a model for domestication, and cooking a paradigm for pyrotechnologies generally. But that was only a point of cultural kindling, for fire was a universal catalyst, never far from whatever people did, and by changing its settings, people in turn changed fire. Over time wild fire assumed new identities. It was tamed, hunted, foraged, fished, cultivated, urbanized and machined. Almost everything people did they did with fire, and fire with them.

Still, fire patterns varied as much as people and places did. In rough terms, the major distinctions follow from the degree of control people exercised over burning. In some cases – the earliest of practices – they manipulated fire by controlling ignition. They could decide the time, place, frequency and size. Later, they could also deliberately control the fuels on which fire fed. They could modify landscapes and in extreme cases convert even sites immune to natural fire into combustibles primed to burn. They could hack, split, drain, dry, spread out, pack together or otherwise transform bulk biomass into available fuel, and thus expand the seasons and spaces ready for kindling, which is to say they could revise the fire regime and shape all the elements that interacted with it.

The possible combinations of fire starting and fuel prepping are many, and they exhibit a logic that is both practical and historical. You can burn without slashing, and burning is itself a means of rearranging fuels, but no one slashes without subsequently burning. Moreover, virtually every fire practice has its analogue in nature. Lightning is nature's electrostatic fire-stick; in

natural fire regimes, people would have seen fire started over and again by lightning (in fact, some cultures will extinguish their own fires and rekindle their hearths from a natural source when lightning starts a fire nearby). Elephants and windstorms trash trees that subsequently burn up and then sprout luxuriantly. Flaming fronts can set in motion a caravan of species, a functioning food chain, from fleeing insects to eager raptors. It remains only for humans to seize the torch and turn the process to their own ends.

In many myths of fire's origin, it is stolen or captured and then loosed and lodged in the landscape. There it remains until people coax it out. This is a good description of aboriginal fire, for fire comes from nature and relies on nature to spread it, which is why hunting and foraging societies are drawn to fire-prone places. With time and more mature toolkits, people could modify the setting deliberately so that the land could receive fire more easily and carry it more boldly. Repeated use made landscapes even more susceptible to fire. *Ex igne ignis*: fire from fire.

Robert Havell, *Panoramic View of King George's Sound and Adjacent Country*, Panel 1, 1834. Note a hearth fire in the foreground and a bushfire in the middle distance.

Aboriginal fire: control over ignition

Some fire practices worked by control over ignition alone. Sites that burned naturally were primed for human takeover, as people preemptively burned or otherwise substituted their fires for wild ones as they replaced aurochs with dairy cows. By such means they could promote the fires they wanted and protect against those they didn't. Typically, aboriginal burning – as we might term such practices – begins early in the dry season and climaxes as the rains approach. And what happens annually is synecdochical for what happens over a longer period of time, as humanity's tamed fires have replaced nature's wild ones (see overleaf).

The simplest way to imagine how people reorganize regimes is to consider two organizing principles, which express the resulting matrix through corridors and patches, of what might be called lines of fire and fields of fire. The lines trace routes of travel. The fields describe places of particular interest for harvesting plants and animals by foraging and hunting.

Foraging by fire can prune berry patches and shrubs harvested for fresh twigs. It can stimulate select tubers such as camas and geotrophs. It can assist the harvesting of pine nuts, chestnuts and *mowia* flowers. Burning can clean out, for a while, nasty pests such as ticks and harvest mites. It can keep thoroughfares open, visible to travellers, and free of entangling scrub. It can create defensible space around combustible habitations such as wattle wickiups and thatched lean-tos; it can expose to view possible threats from tigers, snakes or enemy raiders. It can communicate through smoke, and by means of controlled smoke alert local communities that a party of outsiders is passing through with peaceful intent. More malevolently, it can be a weapon of war.

By means of selective burning, habitats can be made more hospitable to favoured fauna. A good fire can stall a place's tendency towards closed forests, instead refreshing the sun-thirsty browse and grasses that game animals feed upon. In the short term, burning can effectively 'bait' the landscape in ways that draw animals to the sumptuous green shoots poking through the ash (in fly- and mosquito-infested areas smudge pots can serve the same purpose). Over the long term, repeated burning sustains a habitat against pressures to overgrow into scrub or closed forest and thus promotes a higher population of hunted species than nature would otherwise allow. Elk, springbok, chital deer – none

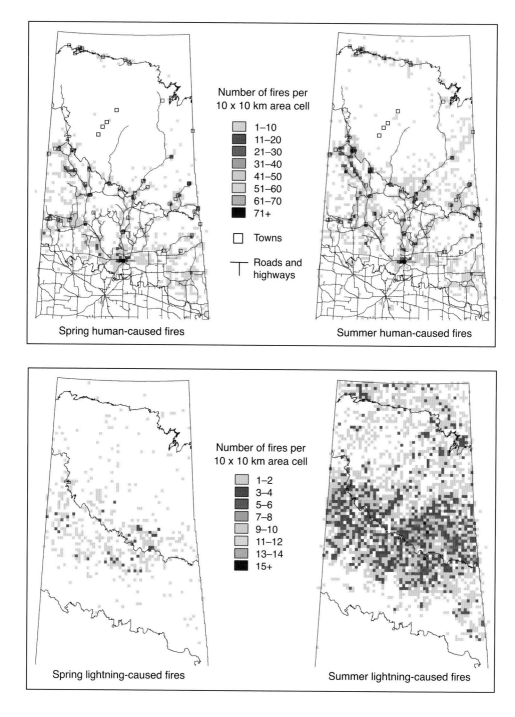

Spring human-caused fires

Summer human-caused fires

Number of fires per
10 x 10 km area cell

- 1–10
- 11–20
- 21–30
- 31–40
- 41–50
- 51–60
- 61–70
- 71+

☐ Towns

⊤ Roads and highways

Spring lightning-caused fires

Summer lightning-caused fires

Number of fires per
10 x 10 km area cell

- 1–2
- 3–4
- 5–6
- 7–8
- 9–10
- 11–12
- 13–14
- 15+

Setting an escape fire. A. F. Tait, for Currier & Ives, *Life on the Prairie. The Trapper's Defense. 'Fire Fight Fire'*, 1862.

thrive in old-growth forest. Seasonal burning – places blackened or greening up – can direct the seasonal movement of ungulates. Trappers in the taiga burn strips that will become routes of travel for hunted mammals over the winter, and hence ideal places in which to set snares.

Most spectacularly, fire hunting can take the form of active drives in which flames serve as beaters to force animals through a gauntlet or into places where they can be more easily killed. Flames accompany spear and arrow. Animals so hunted include whatever the primary grazer might be in places amenable to surface burns. In North America deer were fire herded into tidal peninsulas or into lakes, bison driven over cliffs, rabbits surrounded and even grasshoppers gathered by rings of flame and smoke. The genius of the system is of course that it promotes and renews the habitat that makes the valued game possible. Far from an act of vandalism, the practice is a model of sustainability.

The schizophrenic pyrogeography of nature and people, as illustrated from 1981 to 2000 in Saskatchewan, Canada. The upper maps show the distribution of anthropogenic fires for spring and summer. Note the close association of fires with roads and towns. The lower maps show the scatter of lightning-caused fires, which begin north of the Prairies and show some clustering, but in patterns quite distinct from those created by people.

Many historical records across many continents describe some variant of fire hunting, but by far the best eyewitness accounts come from Australia. The reason is simple. Australia was the last vegetated continent to be visited by Europeans and was inhabited by Aboriginal peoples who lived by hunting, fishing and foraging. Because of this timing, the earliest encounters had

57

naturalists among the exploring parties, who left records that spoke to natural history in ways that missionaries and conquistadors did not. Moreover, in remote areas – of which Australia has many – select practices continued into relatively recent times. Summarizing the fire habits of indigenous peoples in the tropical north, anthropologist Rhys Jones characterized the practice as 'fire-stick farming'. The varied, meticulous and ceaseless use of fire constituted, to his mind, a kind of horticulture. Aborigines shaped the land almost as fully as farmers, but in forms that European observers did not recognize as such, for they used fire-sticks and spears in place of axes and ploughs. In this enterprise fire was a universal catalyst, if not a tool. Exploring artists bequeathed a visual record of Aboriginal burning that is unique in the world.

Joseph Lycett, *Aborigines using Fire to Hunt Kangaroos*, c. 1820, water and gouache on paper.

In 1847 Surveyor General Thomas Mitchell famously summarized the dynamic:

Fire, grass, and kangaroos, and human inhabitants, seem all dependent on each other for existence in Australia; for any one of These being wanting, the others could no longer continue. Fire is necessary to burn the grass, and form those open forests, in which we find the large forest-kangaroo; the native applies that fire to the grass at certain seasons, in order that a young green crop may subsequently spring up, and so attract and enable him to kill or take the kangaroo with nets. In summer, the burning of long grass also discloses vermin, birds' nests, etc., on which the females and children, who chiefly burn the grass, feed. But for this simple process, the Australian woods had probably contained as thick a jungle as those of New Zealand or America, instead of the open forests in which the white men now find grass for their cattle, to the exclusion of the kangaroo.

To complete his assessment, Mitchell wrote a melancholy coda: 'Kangaroos are no longer to be seen there [Sydney]; the grass is choked by underwood; neither are there natives to burn the grass.'[1]

Aboriginal maala hunt, 1930s, in H. H. Findlayson, *The Red Centre.*

In remote areas those ancient practices continued where not disturbed by the loss of Aborigines, invasions of rabbits and sheep, or exotic weeds. In the 1930s H. H. Finlayson witnessed (and photographed) a fire hunt in what he called the Red Centre. 'The blacks' favourite method of taking the animal [maala] is to fire the country.'

The third day was ideal, a scorcher with a hot north-west wind. As we left camp in the early morning for the ground, the blacks were in great spirits, chanting a little song to themselves, twirling their fire-sticks and at intervals giving instructions to the two weeis, who had not seen a maala drive before.

The whole procedure adopted appears to have become standardized and perfected by age-long repetitions. Firstly, runners are sent into the wind with fire-sticks. They diverge from the starting-point along two lines, and, thrusting the torch into spinifex (*Triodia*) clumps at intervals of about fifty yards, they soon have an open horseshoe of flame eating into the resinous and almost explosively inflammable vegetation. The extent of country fired depends, of course, on the size of the party operating, but in the present case when the runners were recalled, the arms of the horseshoe were nearly two miles long and the extremities at the open end which faces the wind, were nearly a mile apart. The country outside the horseshoe is left to its fate, but matters are so arranged that the areas where maala tracks are thickest are within the lines of flame, and upon this space attention is focused.

The subsequent events form three distinct phases, during each of which some kills are made. The fire, of course, makes rather slow headway against the wind, but as it creeps on, all life forsakes the tussocks well in advance of the flame and a steady concentration of all living things is effected. As the flames advance into the wind, the party recedes from them slowly, keenly watching for a break-away from every likely looking tussock, and should a maala break cover within range, his chance of dodging the throwing-sticks is slender. This is the first phase, and it occupied most of the morning. But while this has been going on the extremities of the wings of flame have been closing in and when at last they meet, the action suddenly quickens and the second phase is ushered in.

With the wind full behind it, the closed line of flame now rushes back towards the starting-point, and to the steady roar of the leeward fire is added the sudden menacing boom of the windward one, changing from time to time to a crash, as some isolated patch of mulga or corkwood is engulfed, and swept out of existence in a second. The party now gathers up the spoils already taken and dashes through the leeward fire to the safety of the burnt ground beyond, and there, in line, awaits the meeting of the double wall of flame, when every living thing which has remained above ground must come within range of their throw.

It is a time of most stirring appeal. The world seems full of flame and smoke and huge sounds; and though the heat is terrific, yet one is scarcely conscious of it. In the few tense moments that remain before they break into frenzied action and frenzied sound, I watch the line of blacks. The boys can scarcely control their movements in their excitement; the three men, muscled like greyhounds, are breathing short and quick; they swing their weight from foot to foot, twirling their throwing-sticks in their palms, and as they scan the advancing flames their great eyes glow and sparkle as the climax of the day draws near. It is their sport, their spectacle, and their meat-getting all in one; and in it they taste a simple intensity of joy which is beyond the range of our feeling.

It is soon over, and we go back to the iron wood camp in mid-afternoon to wait for the ground to cool before beginning on the third and final phase. It might be thought that such a fire would wipe out every living thing in its path, but that this is by no means so, can be seen from inspection of the ground afterwards, when fresh mammal tracks are in

John White's drawing for the engraving in Thomas Hariot, *A Briefe and True Report of the New Found Land of Virginia* (1590).

plenty; it follows also from the fact that the whole business had been carried out systematically for untold generations and over enormous areas of country. At such time the burrowing habit is the salvation of both mammals and reptiles; and as there is no massive smouldering debris as in a forest fire, it is only a matter of a few hours before most forms are on the move again, looking for pastures new. But the prickly vegetation having been swept away, the sites of the burrows are exposed and the subsequent digging operations much facilitated. The maala, which makes only a shallow pop hole, now falls an easy victim.

Following up the third phase carried us over into the fourth day . . .[2]

The process could be repeated over centuries because a bond exists between fuel and flame. Spinifex, the spiny bunch grass, must grow outwards sufficiently to provide a continuous cover of combustibles. Such matured spinifex is, in fact, the preferred habitat of the maala, and is in part what limits the spread of the fire, which is restricted to those areas capable of carrying it. The life cycle of spinifex thus coincides with the existing fire regime and sets the dimensions of the burning to follow. Any new patch will burn more or less as the old one did. Had Finlayson linked the growth habits of spinifex to the rhythm of burning, he would have written a complement for maala to that which Mitchell wrote for kangaroo.

The world of aboriginal fire has much more of course. So universal a technology is fire that very little happens without its catalytic presence, especially in societies where technology is sparse and simple. Even fishing has its fire component, as people carry it in boats and shine it into waters to attract fish, and then cook or smoke the catch. Where people go, fire goes – even when they go to places that are intrinsically incombustible.

Cultivated fire: control over combustibles

The further taming of fire required people to advance beyond oblique influence over fuels – say, the outcomes achieved by previous burning – and intervene more deliberately. They moved to a more overt and comprehensive tending that resembles cultivation in order to burn to increase yields of desired flora and fauna, in particular to promote domesticated species. (Industrial societies have adapted similar techniques to encourage desired wildlife. Thus Aldo Leopold observed that 'game can be restored by the *creative use* of the same tools which have hithertofore destroyed it – axe, plow, cow, fire, and gun'. In reality fire is a catalyst for all the others.[3])

The expressions possible are as varied as the tended landscapes available. One variant, fire herding, evolves readily out of fire hunting. Another, fire farming, emerges seamlessly out of fire foraging. In each case, by manipulating the environment, fire cultivators seek to align fuel and flame more closely.

Fire herding (or pastoralism) mimics the migrations of wildlife as herds move seasonally between natural pastures – and the burning of such sites. Just as fires create a mosaic of burning, unburned and greening patches that entice or drive off grazers, so deliberate burning and shepherding can bring a further degree of control to the cycle. The critical factor is the importance of fresh fodder ('green pick') that sprouts on fired sites. The most nutritious and palatable is the newest, often poking through the ash. After a year the dead grass holds little nutrition or attraction. After two years it is often fit only for flame. Under purely natural conditions, the distribution of such sites – and hence the movement of herds – follows the logic of lightning. Under fire hunting, deliberate burning nudges the instinctive inclinations of the grazers by drawing them to fired sites. With fire herding,

Bolos and burning: 'Fire hunting for rhea and guanachos, Rio Chico, Argentina', from George C. Musters, *At Home with the Patagonians* (London, 1871).

Frederic Remington, *The Grass Fire*, 1908, oil on canvas.

the burning is coordinated with the conscious moving of flock or herd.

As might be expected, the variations are many. In the Great Plains of North America herders on long cattle drives arranged for farmers in the Flint Hills to burn prairie at specified times in the spring so that new grass would await the hungry herds (which, not coincidentally, would also not be vulnerable to wildfire galloping through the dry old stalks). But the most spectacular (and famous, or notorious) is the style of transhumant herding common to the Mediterranean basin. Here flocks moved into the mountains for the summer and down to the valleys for winter. Along the corridors they travelled, fires were common and typically deliberate. Sometimes shepherds burned well ahead of the climbing flocks, encouraging a spring flush; more often, they trailed fire behind them as the flocks plodded down the slopes. Since winter was the rainy season, those autumn burns would flush into spring fodder.

It was the art of an ancient husbandry; Virgil and Silius Italicus speak of the shepherds' burning. But because the cycle of

Moor paring and
burning in Friesland.

movement was out of sync with the rhythms of arable farming,
and because fires could escape or be used maliciously, their routine burning could be taken as another expression of the herders'
alienation from sedentary society. Like satyrs, they lived on the
margins and seemed to mock the mores of a fixed society; one
of their cloven-footed kind, Satan, had an overt alliance with a
hellish fire. Still, these were practices emigrating Europeans
brought to the New World, recreating the Spanish altiplano in
Mexico and transplanting transhumance to the Sierra Nevada,
Cascades and Rockies of the American West, where they pro-
voked another round of condemnation both for their louche
behaviour and their lascivious flames, as well as for the choking
smoke that filled the inhabited basins and valleys.

    Even more calculated was fire farming. In truth, very little
cultivation occurred outside floodplains without fire (and even
floodplain stubble was often burned). If fire herding was an adap-
tation of fire hunting, fire farming involved a more robust fire-
stick foraging, and both were exercises in applied fire ecology.
Fire farming organized the cycle of cultivation around the cycle of
postfire recovery. The first year after a burn was the prime phase
for planting – rich in ash, purged of competitors. The second
year was a struggle against weeds and declining fertility. By the

Field burning in the
Black Forest region
of Germany.

third year a plot could hold out against the indigenous biota only
with heroic hoeing and active enrichment.

It is then no accident that the rhythm of fire cultivation is
roughly three years. Two variants are common. In one, the farm
is fixed at one site while a succession or rotation of domesticated
crops follows. In the other, the farm itself is recreated anew around

the countryside. That is, in the latter the farm moves through the landscape, while in the former the landscape moves through the farm. The difference between them is partly explained by environmental conditions and partly by the political economy of land tenure. What both share is a linkage between flame and fuel, or what agronomists call fallow. For most of European history intellectuals and government ministers condemned fallowing as wasteful, superstitious and, since it got fired, dangerous. But it seems more reasonable to pick up the other end of the stick and appreciate that the fallow was not burned to get rid of it, but grown in order to be burned. The fire was not incidental: it was the point. The jolt of flame was, ecologically, what the field needed to be able to grow exotic plants.

Burning in the Austrian Alps.

Such fires required adequate fuels and, depending on whether the landscape was moved through the field (as with field rotation) or the field through the land (as with swidden), the way to get fuels was to grow them or to slash them. On a regular cycle, then, land would be fluffed with fuels. It would be abandoned, maybe subject to some grazing, or a new plot would be felled and its debris spread over the field. If the site could not produce enough fallow, then more biofuel would be hauled to the scene; pruned limbs, pine needles, dried dung, even parched seaweed, whatever might burn and add to the impact of the fire. Over time, perhaps a decade, perhaps half a century, the abandoned plot in the woods would be revisited, re-slashed and burned anew.

In brief, these were linked systems in which neither fallow nor fire was sufficient by itself but only when joined. And apart from fallow burning, the stubbly residue of harvest was often fired to clean and renew fields on a milder level. In a given place the patches and pulses of burning – that is, the fire regime – assumed the shape of agriculture. Fire became as domesticated as flocks of sheep and rows of potatoes and sugar cane.

Finnish swidden, converting forest to field (1877), by G. W. Edlund.

Built fire: constructing a habitat for fire

Humanity's other habitat was the house, or in aggregate, the town or city. The scene goes to the paradoxical core of anthropogenic fire, for the earliest structures were designed to protect the fire and yet, equally, to protect people from that fire. The distinction was that the hearth fire was domesticated and wanted, and the wild fire was neither.

Fireplaces were incombustible: they were often the only feature of a house that survived a general conflagration. The hearth was, moreover, the central feature or focus of the human habitation (this was literally true; *focus* is Latin for hearth). But the surrounding structures were not designed to burn. If they did

Finnish field burning, a painting of 1883.

burn, it was because they were made with the same materials as the neighbouring landscape and so responded in a similar way to drought, wind and ignition. Many built landscapes were reconstituted forests, and burned accordingly. East winds drove flame through London in 1666 as they did the moors of Yorkshire; in 1904 a cold front blasted through Baltimore, causing the flames to run northward and then southeast, much as another front did during the 1910 Big Blowup in the Northern Rockies. As in nature large fires tended to burn the very young and very old, and places chocked with ready fuels; and as in nature, they led to renewal. The burned sites became the scenes for new growth and more pleasant habitats.

Early efforts to spare cities from wildfire emphasized the need to control both spark and fuel. Ignition was tricky since open flame was everywhere, from candles to hearths to workshop forges. But careful tending kept it in its place and away from ready flammables, and patrols at night kept a wary eye out for loose flame (this was the origin of the curfew, from the Middle English (by way of Old French) *covrefeu*, or the command to cover the fire). When fires broke out they were attacked if small; if large, gangs would seek to pull down buildings or roofs (by means of hooks wielded by men on ladders) along its path; and if very large, firefighters would stand aside and wait for the wind to calm or rains to fall. Fuel was no less awkward to handle since wood and wattle were common construction materials, and even where stone or brick could replace wood, roofing demanded lighter materials, which pointed to highly combustible wood shingles and thatch. These were almost impossible to fireproof, were easily attacked by embers and firebrands, and became the primary point of vulnerability.

Different societies coped with the threat of urban fire as they did with the perils and prospects of free-burning fire on the surrounding landscape. The two settings, after all, frequently burned in tandem. Some cities, in East Asia for example, accepted that they would burn, much as they might regularly flood or shake apart from earthquakes. They accordingly adopted a strategy of resilience that sought to minimize damage and allow for rapid re-growth. Other places, such as in central Europe, sought to abolish fire to the greatest extent possible; they tried to make cities impregnable to flame. This made sense granted the inherent immunity to fire of the natural (or cultivated) landscape around them – places for which fire existed solely because people put it there. Observers saw the same as true for their towns, which burned due to carelessness, social unrest or war. Because fires resulted from human malfeasance, they could in principle be abolished through better behaviour.

Over time modern cities have become less fire-prone. The reasons are straightforward and tied, in one way or another, to industrialization. There are fewer open flames, and these must interact with a built environment erected with fewer combustibles and more concrete, brick, steel and glass. The design of buildings, from rooms to exits, must conform to codes that consider fire: interior materials are tested for fire safety, and automated smoke detectors, sprinklers and firewalls are standard features. Thanks to modern transport the built landscape has dispersed, lessening the chance for flame to leap from building to building. Fire protection saturates the cityscape. There are alarms, automated detection and response systems, and heavily

Unknown artist, *The Great Fire of London*, 1666.

machined fire engines along with the crews to staff them. There are fewer opportunities for fire to start, fewer chances for it to spread, and fewer occasions where fire can overpower attempts to suppress it. A large or catastrophic fire is not one that burns widely but one that affects densely inhabited buildings.

When modern – that is, industrial – cities burn, the cause is typically war or earthquakes. Both circumstances stir up sparks and dampen the ability to tackle them. Or, reaching beyond the urban core, fires break out along an exurban fringe, where the built landscape slams into a still wild one. The fires rush out of a natural habitat and strike a realm that, because residents don't define it as urban, does not incorporate the fire prevention lessons gleaned over millennia. Such settings are neither wild nor built, but – too often – only burned.

The range of human practices maps neatly onto the range of human habitations. The one constant is that fire and people are never apart. Hearth, fallow, pasture, woodland, village, hunting ground, foraging field, swidden plot, nature park – all hold fire at the bidding of hand and head, and all, by shaping the worlds people inhabit, shape those people. Environments that are made or occupied will be selected for the variety of fires that is possible; the kinds of fires that are possible determine the kinds of domiciles and landscapes people will live in. Its fire practices thus speak to the values, beliefs and character of a society as fully as its architecture, laws and literature. Fire and people are, in a sense, doubles: know one and you will know much about the other.

5 Famous Fires: An Anthology

Fires have their celebrity. They are by turns catastrophic, legendary, notorious, winsome, heroic and odious, depending on how they interact with the human society around them. Their cultural bond is what makes big fires into great ones, and otherwise ecological-business-as-usual fires famous. Because they interpenetrate so much of human life, each aspect of culture has its own fiery candidates for renown. There are famous fires in mythology, in science and technology, in the histories of the various lands people inhabit – in agricultural settlement, in cities, in wildlands and nature reserves.

Creation stories often cite the moment humanity obtained fire (by gift, guile or theft) as the time when the sapients rose to the top of the food chain, for fire meant power. Stoic philosophy pointed to recurrent Great Fires that ended and began cycles of history. Nordic myth had its Ragnarök in which the world of the æsir crumbled and burned and out of its ashes sprang new life and humanity. Lucretius' epic poem *On the Nature of Things* (first century BC) spoke of a massive fire in the Pyrenees that melted stone, thus inspiring metallurgy. Europe's overseas colonization commences with an epic fire on the isle of Madeira. The modern narrative about the demise of the dinosaurs points to one or several extraterrestrial impacts on the K-T boundary that sparked world-ending fires such that atop the iridium signature of asteroids lies a veil of fossil ash. The heedless burning of fossil fuels seems, to contemporary observers, to be a slow cooking of the earth itself that will end in extinctions; not so much the scorching of the traditional imagination as an insidious steeping, as though the planet were being charcoaled.

All are famous fires of myth, legend, literature and what might be called 'scientific romance'. History has plenty of documented burns, a gallery of champions and contenders; only a handful achieve genuine fame beyond their local region or tribe. What Wallace Stegner once observed, that 'no place, even a wild place, is a place until it has had that human attention that at its highest reach we call poetry', is no less true of fire.[1]

Celebrity by size: big burns

What size might fires reach if more or less untrammelled? They will grow as large as their circumstances permit: they will fill the geographic pixels available to them. The largest recorded fires in North America are, for forests, the 1950 Chinchaga fire that burned through an estimated 1.2 million ha (3 million ac) in the boreal forests of Canada and, for grasslands, an 1894 burn that blasted across perhaps 'several million acres' of the Llano Estacado region of the American High Plains. Interestingly both were the outcome of human ignition interacting with favourable geography.

The Chinchaga fire has become celebrated as perhaps the upper limit in size of forest conflagrations. It stands to fires as Canada does to the national territories of countries – it is famous, in certain circles, as a marker for aspects of Canada that its citizens identify as distinctive, notably its immense estate and boreal outback. The fire started on 1 June in logging slash. Being beyond the line of control for the British Columbia Forest Service, it was left to creep and sweep as weather systems passed over it; and other than weather there was little to halt it. By 31 October, when it finally succumbed to snow, it had pulsed and paused in a long oval through the unbroken boreal landscape of the Peace River country. At 1.4 million ha (3.5 million ac) the burn may very well stand, as its promoters have insisted, for the largest single fire possible in forests.[2]

On 6 May 1987 in China's Xing'an Mountains, a fire broke out that rampaged on an equivalent scale, though with far deadlier consequences. The kindling spark began from a brush-cutting operation and, boosted by the seasonal *burya* winds – the same winds that darken the Beijing skies with dust every spring – quickly escaped efforts at control. For some 25 days it rumbled through the hills and valleys south of the Amur River and, more tragically, crashed through villages, incinerating the town of Xilinji. Some 220 people died, 250 were seriously burned or injured, and over 33,000 left homeless. The crisis became the subject of an impressive documentary by the (People's Liberation Army's) August First Film Studio, which made the burn known throughout the country. But China was also at that time opening its economy and had foreign advisors from Canada and journalists there who took an interest in the disaster; along with satellite imagery they made the fire known throughout the world. Journalist Harrison Salisbury flew over the region of what became known as the Black Dragon fire and was overwhelmed with 'a sense of deep foreboding. I felt I was participating in an inquest on the fate of the Earth.' Through such glosses do big burns become celebrities.[3]

By area, however, most burning occurs in grasslands. Geographers have long noted that the major prairies occur exactly in regions that are level or rolling and that are swept routinely by unchecked winds, which has led to repeated speculations that the landscapes are not simply aflame because they are grassy but are grassy because they are so often aflame. By burning through flashy fuels fires can propagate more quickly than through woods, and by rushing over extensive and arid plains they have less to halt their progress. Fire moves with the winds. Burns can reach staggering dimensions.

A few samples. On the Barkly Tablelands of Queensland, Australia, a single fire in June/July 1974 blasted across 2.4 million ha (6 million ac). An exceptional landscape, surely, but the Llano Estacado burn of November 1894 in the u.s. may have reached similar proportions. An account records that it roared into the XIT Ranch on a 30-km (20-mile) front and continued for four days.

Frank Machau, *Ranchers of the Panhandle Fighting Prairie Fire with Skinned Steer* (detail), 1940, mural. This shows the 'beef-drag', a killed steer pulled over the flames.

Cowboys reported the fire had 3,000 sq. km (770,000 ac); but this was after it had already burned considerable country, so that commentators placed the estimated area at 'several million acres'. The episode repeated in the autumn of 1895 along the nearby Cimarron river, with less land burned within the ranch but more land outside it. Probably each burned as much land as the Chinchaga, but in days rather than months. Still, such fires are less an anomaly than an accident of historical record-keeping. Prior to roads and ploughed fields burns on this scale were relatively common, as equivalents are in parts of Africa today, where satellite surveillance must replace hard-riding ranch hands.[4]

Those figures speak to single conflagrations. Big fires, however, typically occur in complexes; the conditions that favour one

18.01.2003

The 2003 bushfires blast into Canberra. Originating in protected lands, a tongue of fire lashed out at the capital, incinerating over 400 houses and the national observatory at Mount Stromlo.

big fire favour many, and what history often records as a solitary fire is in reality a swarm that burns simultaneously and gets merged into a common image, whether or not the fires combine on the ground. For grasslands, so much of the land burns anyway, often every season or so, that whether the burning comes from one fire or hundreds is academic. But large forest fires occur more spasmodically. The biggest Canadian burning occurs in geographic clusters and clumps every decade or two. (The 1825 Miramichi fire cluster in New Brunswick was as large as Chinehaga.) Not surprisingly, the world's largest fires cluster on the largest expanse of coniferous (which is to say, combustible) forest on the planet, that vast taiga that spans northern Eurasia and North America. There, the opportunities for massive burns are abundant. So while the Black Dragon fire was huge, the land that burned on the other side of the Amur River was ten to fifteen times greater. Satellite imagery suggests complexes that ranged from 12–15 million ha (30–37 million ac) from Lake Baikal to the Ussuri mountains. Some of this occurred in pine steppe, where grasses carried the flames, but larch, pine and dried peat bore the brunt.

The historical record is poor because of poor record-keeping in the past and, more recently, falsified records by the USSR.

An account by V. B. Shostakovitch for 1915, however, sketched an enormous concourse of conflagration in western Siberia, a lowland cold swamp of organic soils and Scots pine, that burned for 50 days over 14 million ha (35 million ac) and produced a smoke pall roughly the size of western Europe. Exaggerated? Perhaps, or perhaps it even underestimated the extent, since the burned area was impossible to measure directly and its magnitude was estimated by the smoke brought by inconstant winds. In 2010 an infamous smoke pall blanketed Moscow; but while large in area by normal standards (3,000–4,000 sq. km, or 750,000–1 million ac), the source fires were small compared to major fires that raged further east, invisible to public opinion.[5]

And then there is Australia. Here is a fire-prone continent in which violent outbreaks appear like whitecaps amid long swells of burning. The 'land down under' inverts the northern scenario: the big fires follow wet years that coat the interior with extra combustibles that a successor dry spell readies to burn. The first monster year on record – the result of recording through state forestry institutions, traveller accounts and subsequent verification by Landsat imagery – burned from 1974–5. Estimates place the burned area at 117 million ha (15.2 per cent of the entire continent).[6] That blotch of burning meant little outside the outback, however, for size is not the same as significance.

Contrast that episode with the 2002–3 season. Some 54 million ha (135 million ac) burned, half of that seared in 1974–5, but among those blackened landscapes were prime sites in the densely populated southeast. Bushfires blasted 75 per cent of Kosciuszko National Park, incinerated the national observatory at Mount Stromlo and burned into Canberra, the national capital. They claimed 10 lives, over 1,200 structures, 21,000 head of livestock and inflicted an estimated AUS$400 million in damages. The flames sacked suburbs. The smoke pall obscured the sky over Parliament House. The fires inspired a roster of state and national inquiries.[7] Yet even amid that calamitous season, the fires that loomed so huge in the public imagination were tiny compared to those that roamed untouched and unobserved in the sparsely settled regions of Australia like packs of dingoes.

Celebrity through saga: settlement fires

Fires become large and damaging when they occur outside the usual constraints built into landscapes and social behaviour. The land is unsettled and fast overturning with clearings redolent with slash or with revanchist scrub. The torch has passed from leashed hands to armies or arsonists, or to newcomers keen to quicken the conversion of raw land into rural. When they go beyond the scale deemed desirable, such burns are deemed wild, and when they also capture the imagination by transcending the ordinary, they can be celebrated.

The history of colonization (which is a kind of biotic conquest) is thus a history of eruptive fire. The European saga, in fact, begins with the first of the uninhabited islands discovered by the early voyages of discovery. In 1419 Portuguese mariners arrived on Madeira and managed to kindle a fire that, no doubt apocryphally, burned for seven years. A single fire? Probably not. But seven years of first-contact burning would certainly be within the scope of comparable undertakings. Similar stories of founding fires exist for New Zealand and Madagascar.

They are also present in the histories of other major settler societies, notably Australia, Canada and America. Australia has managed to fill up the weekday calendar with the names of famous conflagrations: Black Sunday (1926), Black Monday (1865), Red Tuesday (1898), Ash Wednesday (1983), Black Thursday (1851), Black Friday (1939), and Black Saturday (2009), and have had to find other monikers (for example, Black Christmas, 2002) to keep the chronicle going. Surely large fires had happened before the First Fleet arrived at Botany Bay in January 1788, but the melancholy roster does not reflect merely the arrival of scribes prepared to write down what had gone unremarked previously – the tree that burned in the woods unseen – they testify to the changing circumstances that came from the evolving character of settlement.

All, moreover, sent flames down what has been called a natural 'fire flume' between Adelaide and Sydney. The Black Thursday fires that scorched perhaps a quarter of Victoria coincided with the gold rush. The Red Tuesday fires fed upon land clearing in the Victorian mountains. Ash Wednesday's fires ripped through pine plantations and urban bush. Black Christmas and Black Saturday burned into exurban settlements and national parks. Within the peculiar pyric vortex that is southeastern Australia, fires that flash across the land elsewhere on the continent get magnified and pumped with meteorological turbochargers in the form of drought and wind.

The North American scene, so different ecologically, shares a comparable saga of settlement and conflagration. The annals open with the Miramichi fire of October 1825, a complex centred in New Brunswick but that had significant outliers in Maine, thus conveniently linking the parallel histories of Canada and America. The Canadian chronicles continue with land clearing and logging through the nineteenth century, but the most infamous fires came during the opening decades of the twentieth

A Lake States railroad, opening up the American North Woods to logging and clearing, the trans-Amazon highway of its time, *c.* 1881.

century, announced in 1908 by a rolling wave of fire that followed the tracks of railroads along the border, from Fernie,
British Columbia, to Rainy River, Manitoba, and beyond. Then,
from the Great Porcupine Fire of 1911 to the Quebec complex
of 1923, a cadence of conflagrations tore through the late-settled
clay region of Ontario. Fires set for clearing, stoked by slash
and stored in dried peatlands broke free during dry spells in the
late autumn and overwhelmed farms and towns, most of which
were themselves little more than carpentered slash. Some burned
over and again until they disappeared along with exhausted
mines, or matured into brick buildings set amid lands no longer
lathered with logging debris. The fires were photographed and
recorded and provided a useful background for those keen on
state-sponsored conservation and fire protection generally.

Across the Great
Lakes, a similar scenario
for similar reasons as
Ontario experienced
serial conflagrations in
1911–23. The fire that
flattened Porcupine was
the first of the roster,
but the iconic photo-
graph of that event has
also been forged. The
smoke and flames were
painted on the glass
negative.

America scattered its horrors more broadly. The most notorious clustered around the Great Lakes where for nearly 50
years, from 1869 to 1918, a combustible hex was conjured out
of a witch's brew of logging, conversion to farms, and railroads.
The scene achieved its first, and likely most enduring, token

'Great Fires in the
West', *Harper's Weekly*
(2 December 1871).

during October 1871 when some 4,000 sq. km (1 million ac)
burned in the region, with a spectacular conjunction of town and
country. One fire wiped away the small logging town Peshtigo
in Wisconsin while another gutted Chicago, which appeared to
receive Peshtigo's exported flames along with its rough-cut lum-
ber fuels. Both burned identically under the same weather system,
a one–two punch from a passing cold front.

Other outbreaks followed. The 1881 fires feasted on stirred
up Michigan woods and brought the American Red Cross into
the business of civilian disaster relief for the first time. The fires

of 1894 levelled Hinckley, Minnesota, and took over 400 lives. In 1918, fires savaged Cloquet, Minnesota, claiming 453 lives. The cavalcade continued until wood- and coal-fired locomotives ceased to belch firebrands, homesteaders stopped hacking and torching farms out of woodland, and state agencies had the strength to enforce codes and muster firefighting forces. But once again the cultural context mattered. The fires were accessible to print journalism and they provided a dramatic backdrop to arguments over conservation programmes and the creation of public lands that might be spared such lethal outbursts.

Colonizing fires have hardly ceased, and their more recent excesses among developing nations have acquired an eerie double in the form of decolonizing fires among the developed nations. Settlement fires have become especially notorious in Brazil and Borneo, where they burn away biodiversity, consume immense stocks of organic soil, and spew cloying, health-threatening palls euphemistically (or cynically) dubbed 'haze'. The Amazonian fires erupted into global prominence in 1988 when they were linked by the global media to the extensive fires in America's Yellowstone National Park. The Borneo burns, particularly in east Kalimantan, became known because of their valence with the discovery of the El Niño-Southern Oscillation (ENSO) climatic phenomenon, of importance to Australia and the Americas. The 1982–83 season involved an estimated 3.5 million ha (8.5 million ac) of cleared forest and drained peatlands – an immense smoke hole in what was otherwise rainforest. The 1997–8 season in Borneo saw 5.2 million ha (13 million ac) burn. Both settlement movements continue, ebbing and flowing with drought, global market and political interest in relocating populations. In the early twenty-first century Borneo accounted for an estimated quarter of the carbon released to the atmosphere. In 2010 burning in Brazil flooded the Amazon basin with choking smoke. The most reasonable prognosis is that both will continue until their frontiers have run their course – until there is nothing more to burn.

Meanwhile, a reverse frontier is underway in many long-cultivated landscapes as a once-rooted rural population leaves the countryside for cities. Burning that had once been held in check by intensive fussing through gardening, grazing, firewood collection and routine small fires has slipped its ancient leash. With horrified awe onlookers have watched packs of wildfire infest the northern Mediterranean in particular. The outbreaks present a kind of inverted mirror image to those in the tropics: not so much a singular event as a chronic wastage that persists for years. Where countries have suddenly shed tyrannical governments and entered the modern market, the shock has been intense. Portugal might stand as its poster-child, but Galicia in northwest Spain, Provence in southern France and much of Greece have experienced a wave train of fire surges. Landscapes that had for millennia simmered with fire now boil over with flame. These less resemble a plague than a degenerative disease. They appear neither heroic nor fused to a national epic.

Such new frontiers and receding ones, a forced transmigration to new lands or a desperate depopulation from exhausted ones, a conversion to crude commodities or weedy scrub – these are less the symbols of national progress than of national embarrassment. A global media, not a national one, has made them infamous. Their story is less bound to a cultural creation myth than to an evolving global tale of environmental ruin. The real interest may lie not with the circumstances of the fires themselves but with the context of their narratives.

For the developed world generally, the chronicle of celebrated fires has turned elsewhere. It looks, in particular, towards the two landscapes most valued to such societies. One path leads to nature preserves, countryside deliberately reserved from the kinds of settlement that spawned the historic holocausts but one that has paradoxically encouraged a roster of replacement fires. The other path treks towards the city and its unruly fringe.

Wildland fires

These new (or new-old) landscapes have become, for developed countries, the scene of their most famous flames. Because they are nominally wild and because they often occur in fire-prone settings, the parks and reserves frequently burn, and burn with some media attention. But only a handful deserve to enter the pantheon of the renowned. They became celebrated because they burned in celebrated places, or they catalysed reforms in how fires were managed on national estates, which is to say, they kindled a narrative of significance to valued landscapes.

All this returns us to the Big Four of wildland fire, those countries that hold the largest extent of reserved lands, namely Russia, Canada, Australia and America. Each case involves a country with an extensive natural estate and a similar history of colonization during which the indigenous peoples were removed in one way or another and expanses of uninhabited lands fell to administration of the state. Some went into parks, most into state-overseen forests. All had to cope with fire; and when some fires bolted well beyond their control, those break-downs could influence the direction of policy and practice. In this way, each of the Big Four has known fires that achieved notoriety. That is, they acquired a significance beyond area burned or subcontinental smoke palls.

Russia's record is the most poorly known. The 1921 fires in the Volga region, allied with drought, famine and civil war, prompted changes; but the most significant were the fires that surrounded Moscow in 1972 and engulfed it with smoke. The Brezhnev regime responded with an overhaul of its national fire apparatus, from the creation of a fire prevention logo (a moose) to major investments in scientific research, to a formal (and hopelessly unenforceable) ban on open field burning. (At the time of the fires, the USSR was negotiating an anti-ballistic mis-sile treaty with the United States that would have exempted Moscow from thermonuclear fire. Was there a link?) Interest-ingly, nothing equivalent happened after the fires of 1987, or others that followed upon the collapse of the Soviet Union and the steady erosion of its aerial firefighting capabilities. The country had other, more compelling worries. The alchemy that transmutes flame into meaning wasn't present.

By contrast, Australia has displayed a close harmony between nasty fires and political reform. The Black Friday fires of 1939 led to a royal commission led by Leonard Stretton whose conclusions, after a delay caused by the Second World War, prompted the emergence of a consciously Australian strategy of bushfire protection through controlled burning. The 1961 fires in Dwellingup, Western Australia, led to a second royal commission that confirmed the design. The big fires that followed, however, did not prove decisive in shaping fire programmes; they served as kind of fiery (and sometimes lethal) wallpaper for a broader discussion about how Australians should live with their bush. That discourse raged with or without bushfires. Australians debated bushfire policy on the basis of general values and cultural desires rather than solely in response to fires. But bushfires made the choices real and they could be a

Black Friday, 1939.

rallying point for critics. They entered into the Australian political consciousness in 2003 when a conflagration burned into
Canberra and sparked a coronial inquiry that assumed the
dimensions of a royal commission, and with the Black Saturday
fires of February 2009 that did lead to a formally constituted
royal commission. All these were famous fires irrespective of the
ambient cultural consciousness they inspired.

Canada had a different style. Its political character as a con-
federation rather than an integral nation state made it difficult
for fires to have much impact beyond their provincial setting, a
trend that worsened after the Dominion ceded its western
Crown lands to the provinces in 1930. Accordingly, reform has
followed not from individual fires but from serial conflagrations
that rumble across several provinces over many years. The
sequence from 1908 to 1923 was important in shaping enlightened opinion, but not until a wave of unstoppable wildfires
roared across the Canadian Shield from 1979 to 1981 did fire
shape the national agenda. The upshot, after long negotiations,
was the creation of a Canadian Interagency Forest Fire Centre
to assist the various institutions in sharing resources during
major outbreaks, and a mutual aid treaty with the United States
to do likewise across the international border. Otherwise, even
fires that killed or caused evacuations such as the 2003 'firestorm'
in British Columbia were contained within provincial firewalls.

In America the conflagrations of 1910, culminating in the
fabled Big Blowup of 20–21 August, inscribed a founding narrative for wildland fire management. The fires burned some 1.3
million ha (3.25 million ac) in the Northern Rockies alone,
killed 78 firefighters, plunged the fledgling u.s. Forest Service
into perilous debt and traumatized four generations of chief
foresters. The agency determined to fight back. Fire's suppression became not only the guiding but eventually the only policy
until reforms in 1968–78. No fires yielded an equivalent outcome until the combination of the 1988 and 1994 fire seasons.
The former became known for the extensive burning of Yellowstone National Park and the latter through the South
Canyon fire that killed fifteen firefighters amid the country's

Nicholson adit, the narrative core of the Big Blowup of 20–21 August 1910, where ranger Ed Pulaski held his crew at gunpoint while the firestorm raged outside.

first billion-dollar firefighting bill and wildfires that the agencies openly confessed they could not adequately contain.

What mattered, though, was less the size of those fires than their cultural context: that's what made them significant to the wider public. The Yellowstone fires were a mesmerizing event because Yellowstone was a celebrity site, and while they did not change policy, they advertised a revolution in thinking to the public by convincing many observers that fire had a legitimate place in natural parks. The 1994 fires found traction because three years earlier Norman Maclean had published a best-selling book, *Young Men and Fire*. Maclean's was a meditation on the Mann Gulch fire of 1949. But it appeared to foreshadow with eerie fidelity the events at South Canyon, and brought what would have remained an obscure episode in a remote ravine into the national consciousness. It is not the fire but its entanglement with a sustaining society that grants it significance.

The Yellowstone example proved contagious. Other flagship national parks adopted a similar philosophy of management by 'natural regulation' that allowed fires to find their own place. Instead they found their own version of Yellowstone's year of fire. A quarter of South Africa's Kruger National Park burned in 1996, and three-quarters of Australia's Mount Kosciuszko in 2003. While Yellowstone might regard such imitation as the sincerest form of flattery, self-immolation became less attractive generally as a model of management and has not colonized beyond the u.s.

Yellowstone National Park fires, 1988.

Urban fire

With fires in cities a social connection is a given: these are built landscapes inhabited by people. But with fires sometimes as frequent (and banal) as those that abound in the surrounding countryside, the question is what makes some fires memorable. The answer is, those that pack some punch beyond sheer physical destruction. Mostly these are large fires in imperial capitals preserved in accounts by major literary figures as the chronicle of disasters marches alongside the migration of empires. That, at least, is the narrative for Western civilization. To paraphrase Bishop Berkeley: westward, the course of conflagration has made its way.

The roll call begins with the fire of Rome (AD 64), made famous by Nero's presumed insouciance, the subsequent castigation of Christians as the cause, and the rebuilding that resulted, and was recorded by several major historians, of which that by Tacitus (AD 56–117) is accepted as the standard. Explanations of the causes and extent of the fire vary, but it was likely accidental (despite rumours that Nero had secretly commanded the fire in order to reconstruct a swathe of city) and it consumed most of the city over the next five-and-a-half days. That it did not attract more attention may speak to the abundance of routine fires in parts of the city not built of stone.

The Great Fire of London of 1666, coming a year after the Great Plague, gutted the central walled City of London, reportedly consuming the houses of 70,000 of its 80,000 residents. Started in a bakery on 2 September and driven by dry east winds,

Hubert Robert, *The Fire of Rome, 18 July AD 64,* oil on canvas.

the fire burned unchecked until 5 September, when slowing gusts and effective firefighting stalled the spread. The Great Fire found a permanent record in the famous diaries of John Evelyn and Samuel Pepys (along with broadsheet ballads), became a favourite subject for painters and led to a reconstruction that bequeathed an architectural legacy, from thoroughfares to St Paul's Cathedral, that defined the City into modern times – all of which ensured that the fire became a permanent feature of cultural memory. At least in the English-speaking world, the London fire became a historical stele against which subsequent conflagrations would be measured, as well as providing a dose of sardonic wit in which the tally of damages reportedly listed an equal number of churches and pubs burned.

San Francisco burning, 1906. The mostly wooden city was a reconstituted forest and burned like one; note the extraordinary convective column.

Perhaps the next imperial centre to burn was Moscow in the course of Napoleon's 1812 invasion. Fires flared when French troops entered on 14 September and persisted until the 18th; by then some three-quarters of the city lay in ash. As usual, the attribution of causes depends on the bias of the sources, but it was likely a mix of accident and arson. Moscow was a timber-built city that burned like the woods from which it derived; the ability to fight flames was compromised by the need to fight

the French. But a scorched earth was a customary practice of Russian military strategy and it would be simple to move from burning fields to burning buildings, and this evidently happened. When the wind rose, so did the scattered flames, which merged into a conflagration. The catastrophe drove Napoleon out of the city and into his calamitous retreat. In this way the fire entered into official records and personal diaries, and then into Leo Tolstoy's grand narrative, *War and Peace*. Napoleon supposedly exclaimed that the Russians were indeed Scythians, a reference to classical accounts of steppe-dwellers who fired their grasslands to create a protective *cordon sanitaire*; and the practice endured, being applied against Operation Barbarossa, the Nazi invasion of 1941. It even became codified into the textbooks of Russian forestry.

The creation of new cities by aggressive colonization from Western powers (and by those peoples who sought to emulate their style) led to a roll call of famous burns. Some went beyond a scenario of places burned and rebuilt, as Chicago did after 1871 when its reconstruction helped birth a modernist architecture. Others simply came and went like storms. But two proved particularly interesting: San Francisco in 1906 and

Stunned citizens
watch the approaching
fire: San Francisco,
18 April 1906.

Tokyo in 1923. In both cases the prime mover was not war but
earthquakes, estimated at 7.9 on the Richter scale. What those
epic shakings slashed, the subsequent fires burned.

Both San Francisco and Tokyo were primarily wooden
environments that had burned horrifically before. But this time
the nature of the originating catastrophe overwhelmed the apparatus established to cope with routine fires. The shaking kindled
myriad ignitions as lamps and stoves spilled flame; it caused

firefighting to collapse amid broken water mains, disrupted transport and sheer number of fire starts; it broke the social order that would otherwise allow the city to function. The San Francisco catastrophe began on 18 April and burned over three days, after which 80 per cent of the city lay in ruin, some 90 per cent of that damage from the fires; probably more than 3,000 people died. Inept dynamiting and ham-fisted martial law aggravated the outcome, from which San Francisco never recovered its former primacy. Despite efforts to downplay the disaster, the city was the cultural heart of the region, and the story entered popular lore as well as science, becoming an exemplar for the emerging discipline of seismology. Tokyo, too, had learned resilience from a long-suffering history of blazes. But the 1923 event was a perfect firestorm: a massive quake, an offshore typhoon that flung powerful winds over the flames, an inherently combustible city whose capacity to respond was smashed. The combination of shake and bake devastated the region; estimates of deaths range from 100,000 to 140,000.

The unnatural equivalent to an earthquake was war. The Second World War reintroduced fire weaponry (and combined burning with blasting) that left fired landscapes wherever the fighting raged. The London Blitz, while famous, paled in its effects to the Allied firebombing of German and Japanese cities. Fire did most of the damage, for an explosion happens once, while a fire propagates. The firestorms of Hamburg and Dresden achieved a complex notoriety that still lingers as emblems of the moral ambiguity of total war. The burning of Tokyo, Kobe and Osaka, while more damaging, lost out as public spectacles to the atomic bombing (and burning) of Hiroshima and Nagasaki. Compared to fire, which was an old trooper, shockwaves and radiation were novelties whose alien quality made them more frightening.

As cities emerged or were rebuilt within industrial economies, they became less fire-prone. They used fewer combustible materials and they occurred in settings saturated with fire preventing, fire retarding or firefighting technologies, and thus fires could

Two views of the Great Kanto fire (Yokohama), 1923.

Celebrity fire: wildfires backlight the backlots of Griffith Park in Los Angeles, California, 8 May 2007.

not spread so readily. Paradoxically, two countervailing trends have worked against this progress. In one, the city diffuses into an exurban fringe that abuts flammable landscapes; in the other, the countryside becomes depopulated and crowds into dense urban centres while the perimeter overgrows. In both, the fires spread from the outside in.

The exurban fire has become a news staple, particularly when it occurs near major metropolises or media meccas like Los Angeles. Big fires became celebrities when they rushed into Malibu, Los Angeles, Santa Barbara and San Diego in 1993, 2003 and 2007, an almost annual ritual, like the Academy Awards. The most disastrous, however, was the 1991 Oakland, California, fire that killed 25 and swept away large swathes of the Oakland Hills. The phenomenon extends far beyond the backlots of California, however. Exurban fires afflict every industrial society in comparably Mediterranean climates. Similar outbreaks have blasted the outskirts of Sydney, Melbourne, Cape Town and the Provençal landscapes of France. All share a similar pyro-dynamics. What makes for California exceptionalism is the way smoke columns rise over the Hollywood Hills and avalanches of flame fill TV screens.

The flip side to the filling of a peri-urban landscape with houses is the emptying of rural landscapes that then top up with local scrub, weeds or plantation forests that go feral. The process is most pronounced in Mediterranean Europe and has put before the public such astonishing scenes as the Parthenon silhouetted by flame and Coimbra, Portugal, immersed in flambeaus as every scrap of uncultivated land within and around the town burned. None of these has claimed singular status, as London in 1666 did historically for cities, but the larger spectacle – this form of fire as a Platonic type – may well acquire a comparable fame.

PART THREE

Fire Cultured

Like ourselves . . . they see only their own shadows, or the
shadows of one another, which the fire throws on the opposite
wall of the cave.
Plato, *The Republic* (380 BC)

6 Fire Studied and Fire Made

From theology to science

In the ancient world fire had intellectual standing commensurate with its significance in the inhabited world. It was among the early gods, among the first means by which a god made himself immanent, and among the treasured powers the gods hoarded. And if and where not a god, it had godlike powers to shape and explain the natural world.

Fire could do for knowledge what it did for wildlands and dwellings: 'Fire was idea, symbol, subject, and tool. It could rework thought as it did metal or clay. If it required explanation, it could also explain. Fire was the ultimate dialectical tool, capable equally of deconstructing the text of the world into its constituent parts and of fusing them into a new synthesis. Through it gods were manifest, about it myths were told, by it philosophy was explored, and out of it a science evolved that would, in the end, destroy fire's magic, mystery, and metaphysic.' 'Fire', concluded Gaston Bachelard, 'is thus a privileged phenomenon which can explain anything.' It can even 'contradict itself'.[1]

Agni and Indra, the god of fire and the god of water, were the founders of the Hindu pantheon. Hestia and Vesta, the Greek and Roman versions of an Indo-European god of the hearth, were among the earliest and most enduring of ancient deities, and in the case of Vesta having the only temple not aligned with the rectangle of the world but shaped in a circle like a campfire. Huehuetéotl, the Old God, was the odd but hoary god of pre-conquest Mexico. Jehovah, the jealous and singular god of the

Fire rites: Burning Man. Despite what would seem to be a celebration of fire (as a celebration of anarchic desire), the ceremony takes place in the middle of a Nevada playa, it imposes a ban on campfires and private tiki torches, personal art can be burned only on an approved platform, and both firearms and fireworks are banned. Paradoxically, Burning Man testifies not to the iberation of free-burning fire but its ferocious containment.

Hebrews, announced his covenant through a burning bush on Mount Sinai.

More secular philosophies granted fire an equivalent stature. To Empedocles it was one of four elements, the core substances out of which the world came to be. To Heraclitus it was an informing principle, the very essence of that change which characterized the world: 'All things are an exchange for fire, and fire for all things.' To Pythagoreans a 'central fire' organized the movement of nature. Plato famously made fire the essential if unreliable source of illumination for his allegorical world cave. Aristotle's student Theophrastus wrote a monograph on fire in which he affirmed that 'of all the elemental substances fire has the most special powers' because only fire is self-generating. Well into the early Renaissance, Aristotelian scholars considered

Detail from George de La Tour, *La Maddalena penitente*, c. 1640, oil on canvas.

burning wood a paradigm for how the natural world works. This echoed ancient Chinese philosophers, who posited five elements, adding wood to earth, air, water and fire, but then wood was a fuel for fire. Everywhere alchemists turned to fire as a means to understand; *philosophus per ignem*, as they put it.

But as fire became more constrained, as it broke into smaller expressions and embedded itself in the minutiae of daily life, it became both banal and less powerful as a universal catalyst for explanation. It was everywhere yet nothing special, and eventually it became not a source but an outcome of other processes. John Donne recognized the trend during the Renaissance when he wrote:

> And new Philosophy calls all in doubt,
> The element of fire is quite put out.

Yet it took time for pyrotechnology to devise surrogates and for natural philosophers to properly subordinate flame, as the Franklin stove did the hearth fire.

But over the next century fire went from master to servant. The Enlightenment thus did to inherited thinking about fire what industrialization did to its inherited fire landscapes. When the era opened, fire was still ubiquitous in natural history: a central fire powered the planet, solar fires illuminated the heavens, electrical fire flashed through the sky, open flame rippled through field and forest, furnaces and hearths cooked both food and raw stone and wood. By the time it ended, fire had been disaggregated both technologically and intellectually. The discovery of oxygen destroyed fire (or its conceptual avatars like phlogiston) and made it the outcome of rapid oxidation, a subset of chemistry. The groundbreaking explication of steam engines by Sadi Carnot in 1824 made fire's power – its heat – a practical lesson in thermodynamics. Steadily, the removal of fire from its privileged place in thought paralleled its condemnation and grudging removal from landscapes. To have fire-powered machines was a working definition of industrialization; to remove fire from fields was the defining trait of a modern or rational agriculture. The conversion of coal to steam moved fire from being a practice of farmers, herders and artisan pyrotechnicians into the realm of mechanical engineering. The Central Fire held no more explanatory power than the Great Chain of Being.

In a celebrated episode in 1860, when he sought a model system to explain modern science to popular audiences, Michael Faraday chose a candle. Its flame distilled the principles of physics, chemistry, physiology and scientific philosophy, but whereas the idea of fire had once given shape to those inquiries, it now merely illustrated their principles. The candle was useful because it was known to everyone and illuminated so many of the fundamentals. Flame spoke not as an oracle but as a laboratory demonstration. The cavern of Plato's world had shrunk to a guttering candle. Within another century candles would themselves vanish as an everyday presence in favour of electric lights, much as the subject of physical science had moved from burning wood to atoms and genes. In discipline after discipline, landscape after landscape, fire became a second- or third-order epiphenomenon.

The one discipline that continued to scrutinize fire was forestry, and this because state foresters were granted suzerainty over reserved lands in Europe's expanding imperium. They saw fire as a challenge to their authority and a threat to state-sponsored conservation. They obsessed over it, they feared it; they sought to know it in order to expunge it.

Forestry was a graft on the great rootstock of European agronomy, and true foresters did not consider fire a legitimate part of their husbandry as much as something they needed to remove in order to do their proper business. Bernhard Fernow (1851–1923), a Prussian who moved to the United States to become that country's first professional forester, famously denounced the American fire scene as one of 'bad habits and loose morals'. They conceived fire as a problem of social disorder. A rash of landscape burning was something young countries passed through, like childhood diseases, before gaining immunity and maturity. A founder of fire ecology, Frederic Clements (1874–1945), imagined fire as an interruption in the 'natural' progression of plant

Joseph Wright of Derby, *A Philosopher Giving a Lecture on the Orrery in which a Lamp is Put in Place of the Sun*, 1766, oil on canvas. The Enlightenment made manifest – Newtonian mechanics and artificial light from the invisible fire.

communities towards a stable climax; it was something that good engineering could ameliorate, like killing wolves to improve elk populations, straightening out meandering rivers to improve commerce or extirpating smallpox. Free-burning fire no more belonged in wildlands than in houses and cities. In brief, the one profession to take fire *qua* fire seriously was committed in principle to its extinction and further ghettoized its study by making it a source of applied technology rather than a topic that sparked intellectual curiosity and spoke to the fundamentals of how the earth worked.

Still, over the course of the twentieth century the need grew for specialized knowledge, particularly among government bureaus that were charged with administering reserved public lands. Because this was state science sponsored to assist the governing of public lands, it addressed those topics of immediate urgency. These were overwhelmingly matters of fire control, which necessitated physical models that explained and predicted fire behaviour. By the latter half of the century fire laboratories had emerged

The challenge: bringing the rigour of the exact sciences to a most inexact phenomena. The Mt Wilson observatory and wildfire in southern California, 1924.

in Russia, Canada, the u.s. and, intermittently, Australia. Europe evolved a scattering of facilities dedicated to such regional concerns as public safety amid widespread burning in Portugal, Mediterranean ecology in France and boreal biodiversity in Sweden. Other labs such as those of the Max Planck research institute in Germany emerged from an interest in global change, notably the impact of combustion emissions on the atmosphere. New institutions to sponsor fire research appeared with the u.s.'s Joint Fire Science Program, Australia's Bushfire Cooperative

Experimental burn table, Centro de Estudos sobre Incêndios Florestais, Portugal, 2008.

Missoula Fire Lab, u.s. Forest Service, today. It remains the premier wildland fire-research facility.

J. G. Goldammer, the Bor Island fire experiment, 1993. An international field experiment staged along the Yenisey River, Siberia.

Research Centre and the EU's Fire Paradox programme. During its apartheid era South Africa established programmes committed to fire ecology and management for its fynbos, savannahs and nature parks. The South African experiment in fire ecology was an outlier intellectually in that unlike the others it did not define fire science on the basis of fire behaviour.

This research emphasis did not reflect fire's intrinsic presence on the planet or its intellectual attractions but the accident of history by which fire science began as a means to assist fire control. This historical fact made fire behaviour the science of reference: everything subsequent had to relate to it. Fire's ecology, fire's management, fire's social impact – all derived from fire's behaviour. Instead of envisioning fire behaviour as the synthesis or outcome of fire's setting (mostly biological), fire behaviour was identified as the driver in understanding fire. It supplied the first principles from which other fire knowledge followed. This was a curious inversion, in which fire's recent micro-history trumped its aeons-long macro-history. But it explains much of why fire is imagined as it is and what kinds of responses society therefore believes it must initiate.

For a while, this scenario seemed to play out. Fire steadily disappeared from fields, wildlands and cities in the developed world, and its absence became an index of modernity for developing countries. Its study was securely contained within the intellectual firewalls of a score of disciplines. Then the seemingly improbable became the surprisingly inevitable: fire returned.

It returned, most simply, because it had never truly left. Industrial societies had only sublimated and hidden it and, like foresters denouncing what they intended to suppress, intellectuals had dismissively overlooked the pervasiveness of fire on earth. In the poorly developed world it remained as common as seasonal regrowth and spring flooding; amid the fast-developing nations it boiled over, as free-burning flame and industrial fire merged into a contagion of combustion; and in a developed world that thought it had inoculated itself against such epidemics, fires spread through reserved wildlands and slammed against the exurban countryside that abutted them. As the twenty-first

The International Crown Fire Modeling Experiment, a series of giant field trials to emulate crown fires, near Fort Providence, Northwest Territories, Canada.

century rolled in, such outbreaks recurred like episodes from a bad reality TV show.

This revival of flame as routine public theatre has coincided with a rekindled interest in fire's administration and scholarship. In wildlands fire has re-emerged as something to be managed or even restored, not extinguished. Among progressive thinkers fire appears as less a tool for land management than as an ecological process that does a kind of biological work nothing else can. Ecology has rejected rigid models of landscape succession and development in favour of a more chaotic pluralism. The extraordinary summer of fires in 1988 that gripped Yellowstone National Park carried this message to the public, even as the images of Amazonia smoked in by land-clearing burns spoke to fire's dark side. Fire research has expanded outside its traditional domicile to embrace atmospheric and global-change science.

Fire as a threat to life and property, fire as a process vital for ecological integrity, fire as a topic of intrinsic interest, fire as legacy theme for subjects like forestry, fire as something forced into the consciousness and agenda of fields that thought themselves far removed from its reach – the conundrums of fire applied and fire removed have impressed themselves upon an expanding realm of disciplines. The number of publications themed to science has risen in lockstep with the increase in burned area within developed nations, which are also the primary centres for global scientific research. By reasserting itself onto landscapes fire has also reclaimed something of its capacity to act on scholarship as it does on biotas. Today, although no single discipline claims it, it illuminates many.

Pyrotechnology

The narrative of fire technology essentially tells how humanity extracted fire from nature and applied it to new purposes. The usual version points to fire in hearths, furnaces, ovens and machines to heat stone, wood, metal, sand or liquid. Controlled fire lights houses and runs automobiles. It underwrites industrial chemistry. It supplies the energy behind most of humanity's endeavours. It's the fire we see miniaturized into symbolic candles sublimated in electric motors. It's a world of fire appliances and fire engines.

A richer, parallel tradition understands pyrotechnology as a *bio*technology in which we might speak of captured and tamed breeds, much as we might talk of servant species. In both examples one controls fire – gets its desired effects – by controlling its environment. For pyro-mechanics this means sculpting a chamber into which fuel and air, often refined, can be fed to spark. For pyro-biotics it means arranging landscapes into patches of available combustibles and igniting them in suitable ways and times. In the latter instance fire retains most of its natural features, but like a domesticated sheep or dog it has had bred out of it the wilder, unpredictable traits. With fire in landscape this is never the case because complete control over wind, sun and organic fuels is impossible. Even a nominally tame fire can turn rabid or go feral.

The ancient world recognized not only the power of fire but its presence. It lived closer to the flame, tended it constantly in daily life, knew its capacity to remake and erupt. In *De natura deorum* (45 BC) Cicero wrote: 'We sow corn, we plant trees, we fertilize the soil by irrigation, we dam the rivers and direct them where we want. In short, by means of our hands we try to create as it were a second nature within the natural world.' Pliny the Elder noted in the first century AD how much of that second nature depended on fire. 'At the conclusion of our survey of the ways in which human intelligence calls art to its aid in counterfeiting nature, we cannot but marvel at the fact that fire is necessary for almost every operation.'

It takes the sands of hearth and melts them, now into glass, now into silver, or minium or one or other lead, or some substance useful to the painter or physician. By fire minerals are disintegrated and copper produced: in fire is iron born and by fire is it subdued: by fire gold is purified: by fire stones are burned for the binding together of the walls of houses . . .[2]

It is tempting to conclude that fire's history as a technology reflects its intellectual chronicle as an idea. Over time it was removed from the land and housed in specially built chambers, and wild fire became a fire appliance in the way a flooding river can become a spigot. Flame was broken into its basic pieces while artifice progressively controlled both what went into it and what came out. What was called fire was refined into a purer species of combustion such that its power no longer emanated wildly through heat and light but through the controlled machinery of gears and wires.

This is the dominant narrative of pyrotechnology for an industrial and urban society. It tells of a machined fire, of flame remade mechanically into a tool, like a hammer or a steam-powered pile driver. It leaves fire nestled into built niches, much as it is intellectually nested within disciplines. In this formulation fire is both universal and specific in that it appears somewhere in virtually every chain of technological development yet loses its own visibly distinct presence. Ultimately the origins of its applied power is so removed that users no longer recognize the grass strimmer or hybrid suv as a fire engine. They have replaced hearths with home entertainment centres. They know fire only as a virtual presence on screens.

But this is a very recent innovation. If, as myths so often proclaim, the originally liberated fire suffused throughout nature, humanity's second nature has suffused it again though in more calculating and contrived ways. With applied fire people converted stone, wood, water and even air from dumb matter into usable goods. In the end they turned the process in on itself and made a second nature of fire itself.

An astounding gamut of mining operations historically depended on fire. It helped crack rock for splitting; it baked limestone into cement, melted sand into glass and smelted ore into copper, lead, silver, iron and tin. A second round then allowed those substances to be softened or melted and so shaped, poured or forged into tools, vessels, coins or jewellery. Fire was also sublimated into explosives, jackhammers and power shovels. Without fire, mining was just digging, and ore only broken rock.

The process of cooking wood was trickier because the substance is inherently flammable. The principal method is to control
the flow of air so that pyrolysis does not escalate into oxidation.
This is the technique behind charcoaling, for example. The
wood, stacked in suitable arrays (typically a beehive-like mound),
is covered with dirt, save for small vents at the top and bottom
which permit burning with very little oxygen. The process leaches
out the volatile substances to leave a charred wood that can
support glowing rather than flaming combustion, a fuel better
suited to maintaining steady temperatures. In more sophisticated
arrangements those extracts can be collected as raw chemicals.
Similar processes (and an alternative to tapping) are used to extract tar out of pitchy boles and chips of pine, then converted
into the so-called naval stores – tar, pitch, turpentine, rosin.

Military support by fire did not end with such indirect con-
tributions as supplying metal for swords or tar for caulking ships.

Two early modern
fire fights – one by
attackers, one by
defenders.

From antiquity onward flame has itself been a weapon before, during or after battles. Scorched earth was an old strategy by which to check invaders, and it was a common practice after conquests. Although Greek fire, a mix of flammable fluids including naphtha, was a weapon of Byzantine navies and sieges, actual flame was a rare sight in set battles because loosed fire (and smoke) was too unpredictable and might turn on its users. That equation changed with the advent of gunpowder, which made 'firepower' a synonym for military strength and littered battlefields with points of ignition.

Thereafter military pyrotechnology followed the scenario of its mechanical siblings. More and more, the expression 'war machine' was literally true, for firepower meant mechanical vehicles and weapons that relied on controlled combustion to run, shoot, explode and otherwise wreck enemy armies and cities. Victory involved destroying the capacity of a foe to manufacture and fuel such weapons and, conversely, to seize critical sites of oil, for example, became a part of strategic calculations. So the *Wehrmacht* invaded Romania, and Imperial Japan, Indonesia. What iron was to the ancient world, petroleum became for the world of the twentieth century. Armies no longer moved on their stomachs so much as on their gas tanks. In firing oil wells during its retreat from Kuwait, the Iraqi army was not only practising a modern version of scorched earth policy, but one peculiarly symbolic of the sources of contemporary military strength.

The narrative of fire as a biotechnology has evolved differently because it operates in a landscape for which it is not possible to exercise the same kind of control as with a mechanical combustion chamber. Nor can fire be disaggregated into its component parts; on the contrary, practitioners seek the widest range of interactions possible in order to capture fire's catalytic power. What organizes the story is changing land use, of which two matter most to modern societies. In one, agricultural land, open fire that was formerly promoted is systematically diminished as farmers find substitutions for its effects. In the other, public wildlands, fire that was previously excluded is expanding, both by choice and accident, as flame does ecological work nothing else can.

Agricultural fires are not controlled as a candle or a blow-torch is, but more after the fashion of a domesticated flock of sheep. They combust their pyric pasture with the kind of selective consumption that a herd of goats or swine would demonstrate when browsing mast and roots. How such fires behave depends on their setting; how rough or meticulously the landscape has been cultivated, what aridity and wind the day of ignition has. People control fire and extract its effects by shaping the combustibles on the field of fire and by selecting the time and place of burning. They slash, drain or haul biofuels to the site and arrange them to diffuse or concentrate burning. The broadly domesticated setting allows for a roughly domesticated fire. As agriculture has mechanized, the opportunities for free-burning flame have shrunk. Substitutes for the fertilizing and fumigating processes of flame drive it off-site and into engines.

Such substitutes don't work where the land remains quasi-wild or is deliberately preserved for its natural qualities. Here 'prescribed' burns – fires set under specified guidelines – have

Thomas Baines, *Mr Phibbs and Bowman Engaging the Blacks who Attempted to Burn us Out*, 1856. From hunting to fighting: Aborigines harass an exploring party by setting fires.

USAF aircraft of the 4th Fighter Wing fly over Kuwaiti oil fires, set by the retreating Iraqi army during Operation Desert Storm in 1991.

become a fundamental practice in the management of nature preserves in a number of industrial nations. In some circumstances they are intended to emulate natural burning, though with a measure of control. In others they reach into wildlands out of cultural landscapes where they once flourished. While such fires may be tamed, they are not really domesticated. Rather they resemble elephants captured in the wild and broken to halter, or tigers trained to perform in a circus. Their 'wild' nature is what their minders want, since the purpose is often to perpetuate a wild setting; but control is always suspect, and the creature may slip its leash, as a steady fraction of such burns do. The prescribed fire is neither a machined fire nor a domesticated one but a captured ecological process loosely directed to human ends.

There is a delightful back-to-the-future twist in watching the source fire, diffused throughout nature from where it could be abstracted by people, being returned by those people to its source. In the western u.s., full of uninhabited public lands, the prescribed fire has evolved into a curious avatar: the prescribed natural fire in which naturally ignited fires can be considered as prescribed so long as they stay within specified places and within

Albert Bierstadt, *Giant Redwood Trees of California*, 1874, oil on canvas. The giant redwoods, or Big Trees, became the focus of early fire ecology studies in the western U.S., which in turn led to a revision of fire policy in order to restore fire to something like its former extent.

The modern fire-stick: a driptorch used for prescribed burning, Bear Valley National Wildlife Refuge, Oregon.

certain behavioural guidelines. A paradox at best, an oxymoron or a clumsy irony otherwise, the strategy is a device to repatriate fire to its origins. The troubled name has undergone repeated makeovers and the practice (also often troubled) has experienced some spectacular failures, yet the movement continues to expand, because it has to. Fire was never wholly humanity's to mould, only to share and shape.

Ancient city-states had a prytaneum, or public hearth, the pyric equivalent of a village well, to which citizens came to renew their household, sacred and workshop fires and which often came to symbolize the tribe itself. Modern societies have sublimated the prytaneum to sustain their built landscapes, which have erased fire from visible presence. But these same peoples routinely create nature reserves, where fire will persist. Such sites have become the temples of a modern vestal fire, kindled and sustained by nature. From such flames, if only symbolically, people extract the fire needed to restore the old order.

Still, there is less fire than there used to be. Barring a social collapse, there will never be as much as there once was. Even the most aggressive restorers fall well short. The Australian state of Victoria aspires to burn a minimum of 5 per cent of its protected lands annually, but burns at best 1.5 per cent.[3] The American state of Florida – the superlative fire landscape in the country – burned 11,000 square kilometres (2.7 million acres) in 2009 but considers 25,000 (6 million) a minimum standard. A virtual third nature, as a digital Cicero might put it, continues to remake the second.

7 Fire Painted

Any use of fire is artifice, and there is, as every practitioner will tell you, an art to fire's management, whether it be loose herding in a field or stoking a fireplace. A catalyst for so much, fire has long been an enabler of arts. It makes possible chisels, pigments and inks, and around the fire the stories of the tribe are told; yet it also burns books and paintings. It is everywhere on the margins; only rarely is fire itself the subject or theme.

These circumstances – the relationship of people, fire and art – date to the Palaeolithic. The earliest preserved European art is paintings on the walls of caves at such sites as Lascaux and Chauvet. Although done by firelight with charcoal or pigment treated in fire, they depict reindeer and aurochs and woolly rhinos, not hearths or landscapes aflame. It is impossible to render those mural scenes, or even to view them, without introduced light, which until very recent times meant flame. Yet while fire made possible the world the paintings sketch, it is itself missing as a theme or organizing focus.

Vernacular fire survived in folk art. Fires appear often in such works because they appeared so routinely in daily life. Campfires, hearths, bonfires, torches, furnaces, candles and occasionally field fires – all were inextricable from quotidian existence and so appeared in naive renderings of that world. Some societies have relatively rich folk traditions of fire art. Perhaps five per cent of Australian Aboriginal art, it is reckoned, deals with bushfires. Russian, American and Australian folk art has continued to include fire scenes into the modern era, sometimes inflecting into high art and sometimes moving from elevated expressions back to folk. In a few instances, such as in icons of St Elias, fire is part of the motif.

Serious fire art depends on a favourable alignment of motive, means and opportunity. Fire becomes a theme, or an essential accessory to a theme, that interests artists of a particular period. It is something they recognize as art and that can claim the inter-est and respect of other artists. For Western civilization fire art has come in spasms – at times when some expression of fire becomes prominent in society and warms the imagination, and can find some genre to support it. These are moments when a painter can advance a career, build a reputation and find encour-agement by painting fire as a theme or decorative motif; they are moments when fire and art find common cause. Some themes endure, some depend on the idiosyncratic taste of the times, and some simply reflect the peculiar sensibilities of an artist. There are artists who never paint fire even when it flashes repeatedly over the landscape around them, and others who virtually seek it out and paint it over and over. And there are some special occa-sions when clusters of painters, legitimate schools of art, adopt fire as a signature theme.

Among the enduring themes is that of the burning city. Cities, after all, were where artists and patrons lived, and the destruc-tion of their habitat was a notable marker in their personal and collective memories. For Neoclassicists like Hubert Robert the burning of Rome in AD 64 was an appropriate subject. Others looked to more modern equivalents: imperial capitals like London (1666) and Moscow (1812) reduced to ash and ruin. With the advent of cheaper print technology in the nineteenth century, periodicals and a popular audience created a market for images of contemporary conflagrations, which became almost a genre in itself. In America the lithographers of popular taste, Currier & Ives, added fire (and firemen) to their pictorial inven-tory of everyday life.

A standard idiom and a palette of tropes appeared; the scenes became part of an occupational folklore of urban firefighters. The firefighter with hose pointed against the blaze, the firefighter rescuing a victim, the gush of flame through city streets like a torrent over Niagara – these morphed into the icons of a popular sublime. As settler societies planted wooden cities along a flaming frontier, the burning town (often a town that burned over and again) became a convention as expected as the arrival of the first bank or schoolhouse. Throughout, the painted fire spoke a narrative of renewal and growth. But as wooden towns matured into cities made of brick and steel, and volunteer bucket brigades evolved into mechanized firefighting companies, the paintings retired into albums and onto firehouse walls. The most dramatic urban fires of recent times, the burning of the twin towers of the World Trade Center in New York City on 11 September 2001, inspired television journalism, not art. If serious fire painting emerges again, it will be interesting to see if it revives the old conventions or, more likely, falls into genres not accustomed to depicting urban conflagrations.

Other fire art tapped into themes that depended on the idiosyncratic taste of a particular time. The Renaissance, for example, was ablaze with enthusiasm for the Classics, so the Roman gods of furnace and hearth, Vulcan and Vesta, entered into various scenes and illustrated narratives. But the dominant subject was Prometheus. Once painted by a prominent artist such as Peter Paul Rubens (1577–1640), others followed, such as Jan Cossiers (1600–1671) and Jacob Jordaens (1593–1678). Since most art comes from art – it would seem almost as self-generative as fire – echoes can reverberate centuries later, even though later expressions might more resemble the final flickering of a guttering candle than the flame of original insight.

Certainly the Promethean motif enjoyed a revival in the early Romantic period that often identified artists and inventors as new Prometheans. *Prometheus Unbound* (1820) went from Shelley's poetry to the palette; even William Blake tossed a work into the gallery. The emphasis for most images, however, was on Prometheus' horrific punishment for defiance, and, for the Romantics, on his liberation rather than on the fire he carried. And that is the norm: even as a theme fire remained an enabler not a subject. Where fire persisted it did so as an accompanying torch or backstory.

That changed when, during the nineteenth century, landscape came into vogue as a dominant genre and artists had the opportunity to travel to raw settings that were frequently aflame. Many such scenes as wild mountains, rippling prairies and untrammelled bush and veld bonded to an emerging nationalism among settler societies such that paintings enjoyed a popular enthusiasm that would have been impossible in Europe. As artists attached themselves to exploring expeditions, paintings were valued as a record of scenes visited and wonders witnessed.

The reportorial instinct – the painter as journalist – expanded the range of occasions to record fire. From the earliest European contact images included fire, though usually as an implement of daily life. There are images of torch fires, cooking fires and ceremonial fires; fire arrows, fire arms, fired villages; fires in fishing boats, fires in fortified compounds, fires in the hands of wandering hunters – fires as part of a chronicle of discovery of lands beyond Europe. The development of technologies for cheap reproduction of lithographs (even in colour) and the emergence of popular media such as periodicals avid for illustrations created a market for dramatic scenes. The city on fire theme reincarnated as the prairie or woods on fire. What makes the nineteenth century extraordinary for its fire art is that the reportorial style combined with the aesthetic to produce major works by major artists, and even to prompt what might be called one school of landscape fire art.

Not least among explanations for why fire art appears, there is the personality of the artist. Some artists are attracted to fire; most are not. If someone paints a fire painting, he or she is likely to paint another, and most of the canon comes from a handful of prominent artists who appeared at a time when landscape was all the rage and many frontier settings were in fact all a-rage with fire. Of course there are exceptions, painters who created only one notable fire-focused work. Piero di Cosimo painted an allegorical (and solitary) *Forest Fire* triptych around 1505. Frederic Church painted a sombre landscape, *Christian on the Borders of the Valley*

Piero di Cosimo, *The Forest Fire, c.* 1505, oil on panel. This work from the Florentine Renaissance is probably a variant on fire themes in Lucretius or Vitruvius.

of the Shadow of Death (1847), in which the focal point is a giant column of flame – a biblical pillar of fire – that splinters into a cross, and never did another. (It was a case of fire fitting into a religious theme, not a religious theme coming out of a fascination with fire.) Gustave Doré translated words into a lithograph of prairie fires complete with stampeding wildlife (or sheep) for an account in Edouard Charton's edited *Le Tour du monde.* John Singer Sargent did an early twentieth-century watercolour of a fire in the Alps, a singular curiosity in an oeuvre best known for its society portraits. René Magritte produced an almost Dadaist work, *Les Fanatiques* (1950), in which a black bird looks down upon a blazing bonfire, and did nothing further. In such instances fire was a means for the artist to express a recurring theme in a new way.

For some the technique was repeated until it evolved into a recurring trope. Joseph Wright of Derby, for example, became a master at using hidden flame to illuminate themes. Mostly he exploited combustion for its light – its capacity to shine on modern inventions and ideas, as with his famous *A Philosopher Giving a Lecture on the Orrery* (1766). But even when he made fire nominally the subject, as with *The Funeral Pyre*, only a few fugitive flames show. The setting contains them visually as fully as a Franklin stove.

Only a handful of major artists made fire a serious motif, and they belonged to the exploring and reportorial generation that could visit fire along the flaming fronts of European colonization. The most wide-ranging was almost certainly Thomas Baines (1820–1875), who managed to paint veld fires in southern Africa, bushfires in Australia, forest fires in New Zealand and, having learned his craft in Britain, no doubt (somewhere) fire scenes among the moors or hayricks. Most fire artists, however, have stayed within their homeland.

In like manner countries display, or discourage, fire art. Some nations have a legacy, still active, of painted fire, both beaux-arts and folk, and some have none at all. Those with rooted traditions look to their landscapes for national identity. Those with almost no historic fire art seek their sense of themselves elsewhere. Despite immense prairies and a vast boreal forest that can hurl flames halfway to heaven, Canada has almost no historic fire art. (The one significant exception is Paul Kane's obsessively re-painted 1846 evening prairie fire along the North Saskatchewan River.) Canadian artists have sought their identity as intellectuals and their country's sense of its unique character in ways and places other than in its forested outback, and its ingenuity with regard to fire turned to engineering. The Canadians produced fire pumps, not fire paintings. For America, Russia and Australia, however, wild fire was a part of national self-discovery. They expressed that discourse in paint as well as prose.

America's prairie fire school

The famous Hudson River School of landscapers painted nothing of fire, but many of its classic western artists did, drawn into that historical vortex that swept artists, landscapes and explorers into the annually burning Great Plains.

The process began with George Catlin (1796–1872), who painted several famous scenes from his 1831 voyage along the Missouri River as part of his desperate bid to preserve the wild frontier and its inhabitants before they disappeared. One – a common trope – showed roiling smoke and flames along the horizon, with a Native American family watching from the foreground in alarm. Another is a close-up of high plains prairie with the fiery front wending like a rivulet of flame.

> Where the grass is short, the fire creeps with a flame so feeble that one can easily step over it. The wild animals often rest in their lairs until the flames touch their noses. Then they reluctantly rise, leap over the fire, and trot off among the cinders, where the fire has left the ground as black as jet.

Such fires, Catlin notes, are 'frequently done for the purpose of getting a fresh crop of grass for grazing, also to secure easier travelling', but they have an aesthetic no less than utilitarian outcome.

> These scenes at night are indescribably beautiful, when the flames, seen from miles distant, appear to be sparkling and brilliant chains of liquid fire hanging in graceful festoons from the skies, for the hills are entirely obscured.[1]

A third trope moves the action to the centre as mounted Native Americans flee before an approaching floodtide of monstrous flame. Catlin jotted breathlessly into his journal that

> There is yet another character of burning prairies . . . the war, or hell of fires! where the grass is seven or eight feet high . . . and the flames are driven forward by the hurricanes, which often sweep over the vast prairies of this denuded country. There are many of these meadows on the Missouri, and the Platte, and the Arkansas, of many miles in breadth, which are perfectly level, with a waving grass, so high, that we are obliged to stand erect in our stirrups, in order to look over its waving tops, as we are riding through it. The fire in these, before such a wind, travels at an immense and frightful rate, and often destroys, on their fleetest horses, parties of Indians, who are so unlucky as to be overtaken by it.[2]

Fire benign: George Catlin, *Prairie Bluffs Burning*, 1832, oil on canvas.

Fire savage: George Catlin, *Prairie Meadows Burning – Upper Missouri 1830*, oil on canvas.

Fire threatens: Charles
Deas, *Prairie Fire*, 1847,
oil on canvas.

The two polarities Catlin produced set the genre. That hellish on-rushing fire, with the rolling smoke like a thundercloud
and the flashes of flame like lightning, became the dominant
design as artist after artist painted surfs of flame that drove bison,
elk, antelope, wolves, sheep, cattle and people before it. But paired
with it was the scene of a small band under threat. Charles Deas
(1818–1867) painted such flames bearing down on a trapper,
and again threatening a wagon train. Alfred Jacob Miller (1810–
1874) showed trappers and natives responding by setting back-
fires and swatting out the fires on the downwind flank. Currier
& Ives dramatized for their popular lithograph series the more
common response, in which the party kindles an escape fire into
whose rapidly burned patch they would move to ride out the
fast-encroaching front (see A. F. Tait's painting *The Trappers
Defense, Fire Fight Fire* of 1862).

Well into the twentieth century similar artwork appeared
even from the hands of the country's most celebrated painters and
illustrators. Frederic Remington (1861–1909) painted Native
Americans setting grass fires and ranch hands quenching them
with 'beef drags' (see page 77), and desperate cowboys driving

Fire across the border: the Canadian exploring artist Paul Kane contributed an evening scene near present-day Edmonton: *A Prairie on Fire*, *c.* 1846, oil on canvas.

Fire memoralized: Charles M. Russell, *Prairie Fire*, 1898, oil on board.

herds ahead of the consuming flames. Charles Russell (1864–1926) painted the Crow tribe burning the Blackfeet range; bison and antelope crossing a river to escape stampeding flames; and assorted campfires, signal fires and cooking fires. The larger list goes on to include locomotives belching sparks while wild flames and bison race alongside, whole galleries of fire-driven stampedes, and many, many copies and colourizations of the classic images. More recently the revival of interest in environmental matters has rekindled the interest of contemporary artists although, like most artists, their deepest instincts are to imitate their masters.

Russia's Urals fire school

What America did with prairie fire, Russia did for forest fire. Unlike Scandinavia, with whom it shares the taiga, Russia did not domesticate its boreal forest into tree farms nor similarly cultivate fire out of formal art; fire remained a wild presence. Unlike in Canada, whose boreal landscapes are nearly as vast, there was a bond between national identity and taiga, and so with the fires that were as much a part of those woods as bears and birch. And unlike Australia a persistent fire art (and enduring reservoir of folk art) got elevated into something like an organized school.

This happened in the late nineteenth century with the *Peredvizhniki* (The Wanderers), a generation of Russian artists committed to folk themes, portraits and natural scenes that clustered around the Urals. Although fire was not part of the canon and motifs of European landscape, it was prominent in the Urals. What was needed was a catalyst to elevate the mundane and the folk into fine art. That came in the person of Aleksei Kuzmich Denisov. Raised in Perm and trained in the family business to work with semi-precious stones, Denisov began to paint backgrounds for dioramas in which to display their craft at fairs and exhibitions. He became infatuated with painting, and then with fire, and determined to 'become one with fire' by painting its grandeur and power. For twenty years he sketched, painted and composed; he so identified with the region that he added 'Uralsky' to his name. In 1900 he achieved what he regarded as his

A. K. Denisov-Uralsky,
The Forest Fire, 1904,
lithograph. This is the
(vertically) cropped
version that appeared in
newspapers during the
time of the Exposition.

V. N. Dobrovolsky,
Forest Fire; a mix
of Soviet Realism
and Cubism.

masterpiece, *Lesnoi pozhar* (*Forest Fire*), shown at the exhibition
The Urals in Art. Along the way he inspired others like L. N.
Zukov, A. A. Sherementjev, N. M. Gushin and I. I. Klimov, and
while they never explicitly self-identified as a school of art, their
collective output behaved like one. The Urals became as celebra -
ted a site for painted fire as the Hudson River for transcendental

landscape in the u.s. and the bush around Heidelberg outside Melbourne in Australia.[3]

Aleksei had a hard life, occasionally desperate, which ended tragically when the Russian Revolution left him exiled in a dacha in Finland. His masterpiece, *Lesnoi pozhar* or *Forest Fire*, had a similar, seemingly tragic fate; Denisov-Uralsky never learned what became of it after it left for the u.s. Its wanderings began when it went from Perm to the 1904 St Louis World's Fair. War with Japan had threatened to remove the Russian exhibit altogether until an entrepreneurial fur dealer named Edward Grunwaldt proposed to replace the official delegation with a private one in which he would exhibit and sell the works on consignment. *Lesnoi pozhar* eventually won a silver medal and was reproduced in colour lithograph in several newspapers, from which it subsequently entered American popular culture and a ceaseless line of folk reproductions.

Then it vanished, along with almost all the Russian art. Somehow it ended in the hands of Adolphus Busch, the beer magnate. In 1926 it went to hang in the foyer of The Adolphus, a Busch hotel in Dallas. In 1950 it appeared in the Hospitality Room of the Anheuser-Busch brewery in St Louis. In March 1979 the Busch family handed over the work to the National Endowment for the Humanities so that it might be repatriated to the ussr, which was done in a special ceremony at the Soviet embassy in Washington. At this point the painting again disappeared. The embassy said it would pass the painting to a major art museum in Russia; but no museum ever received it, the embassy claims not to have it, and its whereabouts is officially unknown.

Paradoxically, while the original has vanished, its facsimiles abound. Because it entered folk culture it became the most copied piece of fire art in history. American primitives like Grandma Moses painted it, along with a tireless parade of amateur artists. New reproductions, many in oils, appear annually. Like great fires, great fire art has the capacity to propagate.

Australia's bushfire tradition

Australia's bushfires have been long bonded to the nation's identity. Bushfires are as Australian as eucalyptus and koalas, and the community firefighting against them, a set-piece of Australian art and literature. Relative to population size, Australia probably has the densest proportion of high-culture fire art anywhere. Like America there is an element of the reportorial and the celebratory, the urge to record the oddities of an Antipodean land and to identify with its more dramatic expressions. Unlike in America, where the nineteenth-century paintings have a freshness and glory that seems to come from Creation, the Australian bushfire appears more dangerous, sinister and inassimilable. If its conflagrations chronicle the major events of Australian history, the art of those fires traces a record of their meaning.

As in other new worlds, the desire to inventory was a powerful incentive to draw and paint. Australia's natural history was so seemingly inverted – Darwin thought it appeared as though there had been a separate creation – that the bushfire joined the kangaroo and platypus as a curiosity worthy of note. Since

John Longstaff,
*Gippsland, Sunday Night,
February 20th, 1898,*
oil on canvas.

Russell Drysdale,
Bush Fire 1944, oil
and ink on canvas on
composition board.

flames could not be stored in formaldehyde or stuffed by a taxi-dermist, paintings and prose were the naturalist's tools of preservation. The first visual record of an Aboriginal family shows a fire-stick in the hand of a child; few subsequent images lacked a fire-stick. Bushfires filled the background landscape.

In Victoria flames not only scampered about the scene like wallabies but were major events of history and demanded a high style. The roaring bushfire, driving society before it, became the Australian answer to the Grand Manner epics of Europe that dramatized great battles and moments of history. Eugene von Guérard (1811–1901) showed how formal art could frame the wild fury, but only when viewed from afar. The man who brought it close – hurled the bushfire at the viewer – was William Strutt, whose *Black Thursday, February 6th, 1851* (1864) became the exemplar for what came to define an Australian genre. Certainly the artist came to regard the giant canvas as his magnum opus.[4]

Strutt had arrived in Melbourne in July 1850 on the cusp of the gold rush and six months from the first of the great conflagrations of Australian settlement. In February 1851 perhaps a quarter of Victoria burned in what came to called Black Thursday. While Strutt never saw the flames, he felt their conditions and

knew their smoke, entering many notes and details into his journal and sketchbook. In 1864 he composed the vast canvas *Black
Thursday*, which he exhibited in London but always intended for
a public collection. Although a sensation, the painting didn't sell.

For the next century *Black Thursday* undertook a complex
walkabout between Britain and various Australian colonies in
search of a suitable venue. In 1883 it alighted in South Australia.
Over the coming decades it remained in private hands, although
shuttled between galleries in Adelaide, Melbourne and Sydney,
and at least once threatened with relocation to Perth. In 1954 the
State Library of Victoria did what everyone originally thought
should have happened at the beginning: it purchased the painting for AUS£150. (Strutt had asked for AUS£300 initially, and
considered it a loss, but agreed to AUS£200, which one critic
noted would earn him less 'than the wages of a colour-grinder'.)
When the State Library acquired its new building in 1965 *Black
Thursday* went on permanent display, piqued the interest of art
historians and gained the popular acclaim Strutt and early critics had assumed was its birthright. In 1988 it joined a travelling

William Strutt,
*Black Thursday,
February 6th, 1851*,
1864.

exhibition for Australia's Bicentenary, but by the time it completed the circuit the Library was undergoing reconstruction and the painting again went a-droving, this time to the National Gallery of Australia and the art galleries of South Australia, Victoria and Western Australia, before coming to final rest back in the State Library's La Trobe Library in 2004. By now angry, real bushfires were reclaiming their place as a theme of Australian life and politics. *Black Thursday* had acquired the force of a talisman.

Major Australian artists continued to include bushfires, both as conflagrations and as rural burning-off, as a staple theme. The boldest bid to match Strutt was John Longstaff's *Gippsland, Sunday Night, February 20th, 1898* that depicts the bushfires of Red Tuesday. But what really distinguishes the Australian scene is not the persistence of bushfire as a set-piece but the transition to modernism. Almost alone, Australian artists succeeded in reincarnating bushfire into the dominant visual idiom of twentieth-century art. Elsewhere fire paintings survive as popular or folk art but disappear from the avant-garde or high-culture media. In

Sidney Long, *Spirit of the Bush Fire*, 1900, oil on canvas.

Australia the bushfire as serious painting persists just as the bushfire does on the land.

An astonishing roster of major twentieth-century Australian artists painted fires. Arthur Boyd, Fred Williams, Russell Drysdale, Clifton Pugh, even Sidney Nolan – all created major works, often several, on bushfires and burning-off, managing to convey the traditional sense of the bushfire as both implacably Australian and ineffably alien. Bushfires did not simply illuminate the landscape like the bonfire of a corroboree, they *were* the landscape. Flame and char were as much an expression of the bush as sun-baked soils and blistering winds. In no other part of the industrial world has art managed to keep fire in the modernist oeuvre. But then no other industrialized country has so much vernacular fire and such spasms of wildfire that rage through the margins of its cities and can even invade its capital.

Excepting Australia, the great lack in fire art is the absence, in most, of some genuine gravitas beyond the immediate sense of crash and crisis. Whether in painting, literature or film, most works speak to adventure or disaster or a flash of natural sublime, but not to cultural identity or moral drama. It's not the imagery that packs a punch: it's how it makes visible the unseen yearnings, fears and felt reality of a people.

After all, contemporary life is awash with fire imagery. Almost any piece of journalism or propaganda will include flame to catch the eye and animate interest. Some renewed interest has come by an association with environmentalism. Even realist paintings – to say nothing of photographs – abound; but they have become a visual chatter and achieve the unlikely effect of making burning almost banal. Most viewers see those images not on walls or in museums but on screens and monitors. Some of the most gripping don't show flames at all but only remotely sensed hotspots from orbiting satellites like MODIS. They show earth abstractly pocked with fires, like a sweater eaten by moths. For most inhabitants of industrialized societies, that is the fire they know. The virtual is replacing the vernacular.

8 Fire Celebrated

The Cerro de la Estrella rises in the centre of the Valley of Mexico. In pre-Columbian times it was an island, where the waters of Lake Texcoco lapped with Lake Xochimilco. It was here, every 52 years, that the Aztecs celebrated the ceremony of the New Fire. On the appointed date, when the two calendars, the 260-day and the 365-day, coincided, when the Pleiades stood overhead, when the cosmos was poised to crash into darkness or rekindle into a new sun, the New Fire redeemed the world.[1]

The ceremony was elaborate, its site majestic. In all of the countryside around, across the wide-mirrored lake, in every hearth and village, in every temple, in every torch and campsite, the fires were extinguished until every human light had vanished from the evening darkness. Only the illumination of the stars remained. The world – the known world of the sun – shuddered in uncertainty. The dark and the demons crept closer. Only a renewed fire, kindled in the ancient way, the way humans first learned to make it, could spark the sun's return.

On an altar at the Cerro's summit, four priests waited, one for each of the elements, for each of the four previous worlds, for each of the four thirteen-year counts whose beat summed up to a New Fire. A fifth priest ripped out the beating heart of a victim, the mandatory human sacrifice. A New Fire emerged from the sacred implements and was placed in the victim's exposed chest to signify new life; then each of the four priests ignited a great torch from the common New Fire and, surrounded by guards, marched down the slopes to boats waiting to take them in the direction of each of the cardinal points. Ashore, the priests kindled the fuels of a subsidiary New Fire, each overseen by a priestess whose task it was to keep the fire burning for another 52 years. To fail was fatal. From this fire all the fires of hearths, furnaces and temples, all the fires used in hunting, farming, fishing, all the fires of life sacred and profane were kindled. The stars would wheel in their places. The sun would rise. Once more, the world was saved.

Xiuhtecuhtli, Mexican god of fire and time, at the centre of the universe, pointing to the four quarters of the world in the *Codex Fejérváry-Mayer.*

The Aztec fire ceremony was a rite intended to bind calendar and cosmos – was called, in fact, the Binding of the Years. It visibly joined Heaven and earth, the sacred with the profane.

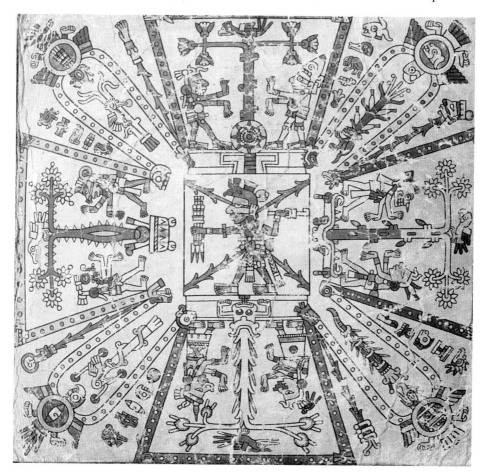

Yet it also joined idea with practice. It bound the symbolic world, the world of mind by which people understood existence, with the world in which they actually lived. Tellingly, fire was the medium for that point of contact. The fire in their minds was as much as part of fire's place on earth as the fires in their fields and woods. With myths they retold fire's story in narrative. With rituals, they re-enacted its role ceremonially.

The mythology of fire speaks not so much to the origin of humanity as to the origin of humanity's power and uniqueness. Fire is not something people invent: it is something they get from nature and which nature – or some potentate that personifies a part of nature – yields grudgingly. Although the details of the myths vary wildly, they tend to cluster, not unlike the way the technologies of fire starting do. And they share a common narrative arc.

At least Sir James Frazer, the great folklorist, thought so. That was the conclusion to his book *Myths of the Origin of Fire* (1930), which manages to be both the most comprehensive compilation on the topic and one of the dullest tomes every written. From his dense inventory Frazer concluded that in myth, fire's putative origin in lightning ('fire from Heaven') is common, while fire from volcanoes is all but absent. The greatest blessing conferred by fire was the opportunity to cook food. All stories of fire's capture follow three stages: a Fireless Age, an Age of Fire Used, and an Age of Fire Kindled. The greatest want in the first was the unavailability of cooked food, which 'suggests that the craving for hot food is a natural instinct of the human organism, for which physiological causes may probably be assigned by science'. The organizing theme of the second was the desperate need to keep fire perpetually alight. The conceit of the third was the capacity to extract fire from nature more or less at will. The shared technologies for drilling and striking stones no doubt accounts for the invention. Despite their 'fantastic features', Frazer thought the myths 'probably contain a substantial element of truth'.[2]

The fundamental truth is that they retell symbolically, if refracted through a hall of naturalist mirrors, the story of how people acquired fire and became what they are. That so many concentrate that power into cooking is suggestive, for as Claude Lévi-Strauss has argued, the distinction between raw and cooked is the divide between the wild and the cultured. Fire is the paradigm – the hearth, as it were – for the capacity of humanity to remake first nature into second and further, to endow it with symbolic meaning. To cook is to transmute through artifice, and to relate myths is to transmute with tropes that rely on signs, emblems, types and symbols. Even in the realm of abstraction fire is recognized as both transformative and generative.

While the myths themselves are endlessly iterative, or as Lévi-Strauss observed, re-knot in one place even as they unravel in another, some themes seem constant. One is how often fire is hoarded. Fire means power, and its possession by humanity could upset the whole balance of power on earth. So it is not given freely, but stolen or acquired by guile or even through violence by assorted cultural heroes. The theme is well known in Western civilization through the various versions of the Prometheus story, but elsewhere it takes the form of crafty thieves, or of eagles, coyotes, rabbits, woodpeckers, spiders or toads. In the usual climax people seize fire – power – and the future. But in some they are warned of nemesis or experience it. In a Burmese legend, the Great Father refuses to bestow fire because it is a Faustian bargain that would cause 'many misfortunes'. In many the perpetrator is punished. But once released, the fire is never reclaimed or, save in rare variants, extinguished.

Even the best-known myths are, like fire, shape-shifters. According to Hesiod's *Theogony* (*c.* 700 BC), Zeus the Cloud-Gatherer withheld fire from mortal man. He had, after all, fought for supremacy with the aid of lightning and, through lightning, with fire. Flames had swept the Cretan battleground between the Olympians and the Titans. But the Titan Prometheus, who had sided with the Olympians, sympathized with the pathetic humans, pilfered some of Zeus' heavenly fire, and carried it to earth in a stalk of fennel – a herb often used as a slow match in ancient times, and possibly an echo of the reed that symbolized the Sumerian god of fire. For this rash act Zeus punished both giver and receiver. To empowered man Zeus sent woman in the form of Pandora, whose mindless curiosity unleashed a host of evils. To Prometheus, rumoured to know the identity of him prophesied to overthrow Zeus, Zeus added cruelty to fury by chaining the traitorous Titan to a peak in the Caucasus Range. Each day without fail an eagle would appear before the hapless Prometheus and devour his liver; each night the organ would grow whole again; and so daily Zeus' rage smouldered and Prometheus' defiance swelled until after thirty or forty thousand years Hercules arrived to break the chains. It was this version that was explored in the famous ancient tragedy *Prometheus Bound*, and it was this vision of the rebellious hero that attracted the Romantics.

Plato offered a more philosophical version. In the Socratic dialogue *Protagoras* he described how the gods fashioned mortal creatures from compounds of earth and fire. Creation took place underground at the direction of Hephaestus, god of the forge, and Athena, goddess of the arts. Once the creatures had been rudely fashioned the gods assigned Prometheus and his brother Epimetheus the duty of refining them and delivering them to the surface. As the etymology of their names suggests, Prometheus could think ahead; Epimetheus, only after. When the time came to equip the created beasts with their requisite powers and talents, Epimetheus convinced his brother that he could handle the task. Foolishly, Epimetheus distributed the valuable but limited skills to the animals as they appeared. By the time humans arrived, there was nothing left. Since the day fast approached when they must disgorge the finished creatures to the surface, there was no time to rectify the bungled creation.

But Prometheus was friendly to humanity, and he reasoned that if humans had fire and the mechanical skills allied to it, they could survive. Zeus' warders closely guarded the Olympian fire, so Prometheus stole into the workshop of Hephaestus and removed fire from the forge. (Hephaestus himself and his fire had descended from the heavens after Zeus had hurled him into banishment, crippling him in the process. In this way the originating fire could still trace its pedigree to lightning, not the forge.) Thus Prometheus could claim that he founded all the

Jan Cossiers, *Prometheus*, c. 1637, oil on canvas.

arts of men, and Plato could explain human dominance on the basis of pyrotechnology.[3]

Such was the symbolism of words. A parallel symbolism resided in deeds, coded into rituals and ceremonies. They too joined idea with act, much as the smoke of sacrificial burned offerings bound earth to Heaven. And they too assumed many forms, amid which can be found some enduring themes.

The sacred and the profane merged in the tradition of the perpetual fire. It could symbolize the deity or be his manifestation, or at least serve as a means of ritual bonding. Whether on Mount Sinai or the altar of the Temple, or in the temples of Zoroaster or Hestia, the fire would burn ceaselessly, always maintained, never mingled with fire from any other source. To allow it to go out or become polluted was sacrilege and a capital crime. 'The fire on the altar shall be kept burning on it, it shall not go out', Leviticus intoned. When Nadab and Abihu bring 'strange fire' before the altar, a devouring fire from the Lord destroys them. When peoples migrated, they bore their core fire with their train. Colonists, ambassadors and armies carried the brands of their sacred fires when they departed. The Israelis and Alexander the Great carried sacred flames before them. Greek colonies kept alive fire from the mother city to kindle their hearths.

In the ancient Mediterranean, Vesta and Vulcan were the two Olympian deities of fire, standing for hearth and furnace, home and work, the fiery welds between the sacred and the profane. They had their public counterparts in the temple and the prytaneum, which were originally one and the same. The first was the centre of religion and the other a public utility. In truth, the symbolic and the practical were drawn to (and from) the same foundational flames.

Among Indo-Europeans the perpetual fire on the hearth was the centre of family rites as the perpetual fire in the temple was for communal worship. Birth, death, marriage, servitude, adoption: all such binding rituals took place before the hearth, or with tokens from the hearth fire. Families sealed marriages and nations sealed treaties by mingling fires; newborn children

Christian Dietrich, *The Temple of Vesta at Tivoli*, 1745–50, oil on canvas. A contrast of water wild and (within the circular colonnaded temple) fire tamed.

were named before the hearth; new members (and even live-stock) entered a family by circumambulating the hearth fire; exiles were banished from its presence. An extinguished fire was rekindled from the communal source, not a neighbour's. A new owner took legal possession of a house by lighting its hearth fire. The authority of a father derived from the family fire, and of a king from its collective counterpart. The family gods were the gods of the hearth.

Fire symbolism had its ecology and its politics. The pre-ferred fuel was oak, the tree most sacred to the sky gods – Zeus, Jupiter, Thor, Perun – because it was, in temperate and Mediter-ranean Europe, the tree most often struck by lightning. (While oaks constitute 11 per cent of forests, they absorb 70 per cent of lightning hits. By contrast the laurel is rarely struck, which ex-plains why laurel wreaths were awarded to heroes and emperors.) The fire thus established a lineage of authority from heaven to earth. The ruler – father, king, pontifex maximus – was the rep-resentative of the fire god and oversaw the transferred fire.

The core fires in hearth, temple or prytaneum were all vari-ants of the notion of perpetual flame. Its most famous expression is surely the sacred fire of Rome, which joined hearth and state. Here politics, social practice and allegory made a fire triangle with real cultural clout. Here was the home fire enlarged to the scale of empire. The fire burned inextinguishably in the temple under the care of a cadre of vestal virgins. As with the fire, so with its tending, for while in principle under the direction of the pater-familias, practice devolved on daughters as another chore of the household. So great were the household burdens, symbolized by tending the fire, that it is likely that one daughter was obliged to remain unmarried until after the death of her parents. The Vestal fire expanded this ritual to the level of state religion. Leading families each contributed a daughter of age six to ten to tend the holy fire. The vestal virgins numbered between four and six and their service extended for a period of 30 years, after which the woman could return to society, her vows of chastity discharged. Celibacy was at first an assurance that the woman would remain in the household; later it became a symbol of the purity of the fire that she tended. Unfaithfulness either through illicit sex or the extinction of the fire was severely punished, even to the point of being buried alive. The vestals thus remained under the *patria potestas* of the king or pontifex maximus – as daughters, not concubines. The *ignis vestae* was the family hearth fire writ large: purified, perpetual. From it on the first day of March the citizens of Rome renewed their domestic fires.

The shrine of Vesta was the oldest Roman temple, and the only one that did not have its four sides correspond to the four cardinal points. Instead it, alone, was round, and it alone had no specific time of inauguration but had always been. Technically the shrine was an *aedes sacra*, not a *templum*. It was the source, the font of fire, such that Rome's temples derived from it, as did the sacred fires on their altars. If the Vestal fire failed, it had to be rekindled according to a special protocol. Georges Dumézil observed:

> The temple of Capitoline Jupiter, the shields of the Salii,
> and the perpetual fire of the house of Vesta: three signs,
> three chronological stages of the promise by which Rome
> lived . . . The fire was regarded as the most ancient.[4]

There were fires in field as well as furnace, and these too acquired their symbolism and ceremonial forms. Again, Europe offers the fullest panorama, and again the record is due to the labours of Frazer the folklorist. As always the originating fire is the source from which all others descend.

This is the 'need-fire', sometimes known in England as the 'wild-fire', in Germany as the 'emergency fire' (*Notfeuer*) and among Slavs as the 'living fire'. The need-fire was the fire of nature captured and tamed. The essence of its ritual is to recreate the original act by which the community obtained fire and to use this renewed, pure fire to fight off threats to the group. The ceremony was enacted during times of crisis.

The kindling of the need-fire came with strict prescriptions, although these varied from place to place. Sometimes the oldest resident of the village would set it, sometimes newlyweds, occasionally a naked couple; they were outfitted with primitive technology – usually rubbing sticks – whatever seemed best to recall or recreate the initial capture of fire. All existing fires were extinguished, to be reset from the need-fire (a variant of the ritual relied on a random fire started by lightning).

The rekindling of fire on the land assumed many local forms. But the ceremonial core was to have the new fire purify and fertilize the community and to prolong those benefits by using the need-fire to rekindle rural hearth fires as well. From the need-fire the participants ignited a great bonfire into which they sometimes threw effigies of witches or on which they burned animals like cattle or witch-identified creatures like cats ('bonfire' derives from the term *bone fire*). Through the bonfire's smoke and over its ebbing flames or coals they passed their flocks – cattle stricken by murrain most commonly; but also pigs, geese and horses in set order. Then they passed themselves. Next they carried the flame and smoke with torches through the countryside, through their fields, orchards and pastures. The ashes were sometimes scattered over the ground, and sometimes pressed upon their faces. They carried the embers or tapers to their homes to reignite the hearth, keeping the extinguished brand in the house as a talisman against lightning, wildfire and witchcraft.

Such ceremonies state symbolically exactly what fire, in the hands of humanity, was understood to do ecologically. They promoted the good and purged the bad. They made the world more habitable.

The need-fire was, as its name suggests, a response to an emergency. But as fire became a routine feature of farmed and pastured landscapes, so fire ceremonies joined an agricultural almanac, kindled regularly according to seasonal rhythms and integrated into a sacred liturgy. Over time these essentially pagan rites became baptized into Christian forms.

Six major ceremonies emerged, two fixed to the annual cycling of the Sun, two bonded to the cycles of herding and two abstracted from seasons for planting. One pair, the fires of Midwinter and Midsummer, correspond to times of maximum solar waning and waxing. A second pair – the fires of Beltane (May Day) and Halloween – correspond to the seasons when the herds migrate between winter and summer pastures, which is to say, when graziers are likely to fire the grasses and heath to stimulate new growth. The third, allied to spring preparations for rousing field and paddock to life, are also the times for burning fallow. These practices became Christianized into the Lenten and Easter fire festivals.

Allow for lots of local variation. Yet some patterns are apparent. The spring and summer fire festivals were generally more lively and widespread than those of autumn and winter. Rough weather, for example, drove the Midwinter fire into houses, where it became the Yule log, while the hilltop blazes that lit the Midsummer sky became the time to renew the hearth fire. Spring and summer, moreover, allowed for the broadcasting of fire by torch procession, by flaming wheels rolled down hillsides, by fiery disks tossed into the air and by the saturating of hilltops and crossroads with bonfires. In 1682 Sir Henry Piers wrote of the Midsummer fires in Ireland: 'a stranger would go near to imagine the whole country was on fire'.[5]

In a symbolic sense it was. The ceremonies not only bore witness to the ecological power of fire but to the need for its social regulation: no community could long tolerate promiscuous or random burning. Rituals helped prescribe where and by

Henryk Siemiradzki, *Night on the Eve of Ivan Kupala (St John the Baptist), c.* 1880s, oil on canvas. The Feast of Ivan Kupala is celebrated at the summer solstice.

whom fires could be set. There is every reason to believe that the great fire ceremonies only codified into sanctified rite and a sacred almanac what people had previously done openly, and what in many places they still did. Yet once transmuted into symbol fire could enter a cognitive ecology in which it interacted with imagery, mythology and emblems that were far removed from the reality of phosphorus released by burning pine, ticks and mites driven from surface litter, or sheep and cattle fumigated by smoke. To pass 'between two fires' referred to a test of belief or character, not a literal walk between purgative flames.

These core rites became assimilated into Christianity before later yielding to secularism. Much as the Jews had fought with Canaanite fire cults and Zoroastrianism, so now Christians warred against the fire rites of pagan Indo-Europeans; and just as Judaism assimilated elements from their rivals, so too did Christianity. Candle or lamp burned in tribute to the altar fire. The Church absorbed fire ceremonies into its sacred liturgy, baptizing the Midsummer and Midwinter fires into the feasts of St John the Baptist and Christmas, the fires of spring into the rite of Lent and Easter, the autumn fire into All Hallows Eve. Christmas log and Paschal candle replaced the pagan Yule log and the new fire. Missionaries condemned burned offerings, and substituted heretics for witches. In 734 a synod of prelates and nobles under St Boniface included the need-fire in its Index of Superstitions and Heathenish Observances and forbade its practice. The ban was widely ignored and in practice the Church continued to remake the ceremonies in its own image so that priests even oversaw the rites and by a process of symbolic transubstantiation carried brands from the purified fire back to rekindle the altar fire. Extinguishing the old ceremonies was difficult and did not occur until industrialization removed open burning from the land. Lady Wilde wrote a vivid account from mid-nineteenth century Ireland that can serve as a coda for millennia.

> In ancient times the sacred fire was lighted with great
> ceremony on Midsummer Eve; and on that night all the
> people of the adjacent country kept fixed watch on the

western promontory of Howth, and the moment the first
flash was seen from that spot the fact of ignition was
announced with wild cries and cheers repeated from village
to village, when all the local fires began to blaze, and Ireland
was circled by a cordon of flame rising up from every hill.
Then the dance and song began round every fire, and the
wild hurrahs filled the air with the most frantic revelry.
Many of these ancient customs are still continued, and the
first are still lighted on St John's Eve on every hill in Ireland.
When the fire has burned down to a red glow the young
men strip to the waist and leap over or through the flames;
this is done backwards and forwards several times, and he
who braves the greatest blaze is considered the victor over
the powers of evil, and is greeted with tremendous applause.
When the fire burns still lower, the young girls leap the
flame, and those who leap clean over three times back and
forward will be certain of a speedy marriage and good luck
in after-life, with many children. The married women then
walk through the lines of the burning embers; and when
the fire is nearly burnt and trampled down, the yearling
cattle are driven through the hot ashes, and their back is
singed with a lighted hazel twig. These rods are kept safely
afterwards, being considered of immense power to drive the
cattle to and from the watering places. As the fire diminishes
the shouting grows fainter, and the song and the dance
commence; while professional story-tellers narrate tales of
fairy-land, or of the good old times long ago, when the
kings and princes of Ireland dwelt amongst their own people,
and there was food to eat and wine to drink for all comers
to the feast at the king's house. When the crowd at length
separate, every one carries home a brand from the fire, and
great virtue is attached to the lighted *brone* which is safely
carried to the house without breaking or falling to the
ground. Many contests also arise amongst the young men;
for whoever enters his house first with the sacred fire brings
the good luck of the year with him.[6]

Lady Wilde thought the ceremony derived from the more ancient fires of Baal. What is undeniable is that in industrial societies those open fires have themselves transmigrated into still less tangible forms. Increasingly fire is something experienced on a monitor or screen; ceremonies are further abstracted into virtual expressions or simulations. The fire floats free, like those tongues of flame that break away from the mass of combustion and momentarily soar upward, their originating source lost. Scholars place symbol upon symbol, following the flames up rather than looking down to the fuel that sustains them and the practices that once grounded those flames in a world of fire-catalysed ecology.

Even today some ceremonies survive, of which the great Las Fallas fire festival in Valencia may be the most prominent and which survives because it has become a tourist attraction. The Midsummer (or St John's Eve) fire continues in Greece and as Ivan Kupala Day in Russia, and in recent years a seeming nostalgia for tribal identities – part of the national deconstruction of Europe, perhaps – has witnessed renewed Midsummer fires in Finland and a Beltane fire in Scotland. These, too, segue into tourism. But open fires have mostly disappeared into machines or been banished by edict. Concerns over public safety and air

The secularization of the fire ceremony: Joseph Wright of Derby, *La Girandola at Castel Sant'Angelo, Rome*, 1779.

Cauldron containing the Olympic flame rises above Aboriginal Australian torch bearer Cathy Freeman during the opening ceremony of the Sydney 2000 Olympic Games.

quality are steadily extinguishing even celebratory bonfires. Such seasonal rituals as burning autumn leaves and firing piles of spring prunings are also being carried away with the ebb tide of lost flame.

The story of Burning Man provides an enlightening coda. The event originated in San Francisco, California, with the intent of erecting and then burning a 12-metre-high (40-ft) wooden effigy. For four years the statue went up in flames at nearby Baker Beach. Then officials demanded the practice end and in 1990 the ceremony relocated to Black Rock, Nevada, where the fire could flame its worst amid an incombustible salt playa. The invented ceremony, centred on a 'fire conclave', draws over a thousand participants. But the exercise in anarchy has also relearned the old wisdom that it is easier to start a fire than to stop one, and that control over fire often means control over people. Twice Burning Man has been prematurely (and deliberately) kindled.[7]

The sense of Burning Man as a symbol has substance. Embedded in the ritual is a realization that humanity's identity is bound to that of fire. Each depends on the other. Before people could control fire, they had to control themselves.

PART FOUR

Fire Today

What we call fire conventionally is not fire.
Theophrastus (*c.* 371–287 BC), *De Igne*

Currier & Ives, *Prairie Fires of the Great West*, c. 1872. From the trapper's escape fire to the locomotive's caged one: a restructuring of fire geography and dynamics, dividing new dominions of the burned and the unburned.

John McColgan, *Elk Bath*, 2000. Fire pristine in the Bitterroot National Forest, Montana.

9 The Great Disruption

The more people adapted fire to new circumstances the more fire they possessed, and the greater their need for fuel. The living world could only supply so much. If people harvested more wood fuel for hearth and furnace, if they shortened the cycle of fallowing, if they exhausted new lands available for conversion by fire, if they continued to extract more than the natural world could restore in a timely way, then the landscape degraded. Burning became a kind of biotic strip mining; as the great botanist Carl Linnaeus observed in the eighteenth century, the world would have rich parents and poor children. If humanity's power derived from its control over combustion, then it could only expand that firepower by finding another pool of fuel.

It discovered that source in fossil biomass. Although these acted as though they were new landscapes, they were actually the landscapes of the past long buried and now excavated. But these fuels were different in that they could not be strewn over fields like weeds or slashed wood or pine needles raked out of forests. They had to burn in mechanical chambers and their energy – heat, light, power – had to be transmitted to humanity's various habitations indirectly. That was the pattern overall. Fuels were extracted from the geologic past, burned in the present and their effluent dispatched to the geologic future. Apart from noxious air pollution – which was no less a feature of burning peat or wood – the ill effects of the new combustion were displaced from the present into another time and place.

So pervasive is fire on earth, and so fundamental is it to humanity, that a change in how the planet's monopolist species uses combustion will cascade through almost every aspect of the biosphere, as well as the atmosphere and even the geosphere. The perception has grown that humanity had accordingly gone beyond the usual dynamics of what behavioural scientists call niche construction and become a global geologic force, which deserves to have its own geologic epoch, the Anthropocene. Advocates further identify a second phase that has occurred since the Second World War – what has been termed the Great Acceleration.

The Anthropocene maps onto what is loosely known as industrialization. For fire history, 'industrialization' is a comprehension algorithm for the shift in fuels from surface biomass to fossil biomass, with all that means for how humanity applies and withholds fire on the land. Usefully, this definition agrees with the general culture's sense of the Industrial Revolution, which it has long identified with William Blake's 'dark satanic mills' belching soot from combusted coal. In fact, all the Anthropocene's potential environmental maladjustments – the onset of

Fire's industrial landscape: Philip James de Loutherbourg, *Coalbrookdale by Night*, 1801, oil on canvas.

global warming, the explosion of human population, modern planetary pollution, the triggering of mass extinctions – align with a relatively simple index of industrial fire. It seems that 200 years is accomplishing what had taken the Pleistocene over two million, and the Mesozoic over 200 million. The Anthropocene is the epoch of anthropogenic fire.

The pyric transition

The Industrial Revolution – emerging during the age of political revolutions – fundamentally rewired the dynamic of fire on earth. Fossil fuels have promised an almost unbounded source of combustibles not constrained by season, place or biota. Humanity's fires can burn winter and summer, night and day, through drought and deluge, amid desert, tundra, tropical rainforest, boreal woodland, temperate grassland – the conditions that have shaped fire's behaviour and effects for hundreds of millions of years have no effect on combustion conducted in engines and furnaces and distributed covertly. Fire has become dissociated from its ecological foundations. Humanity's firepower has become more diffuse, sublimated, potent and unchecked.

The reason is that the new fuels do not burn openly on the land. Instead they combust in special chambers. They created power that had to be applied indirectly through machines, transmitted by electrical lines or used to create chemicals to be transported outside traditional biogeochemical cycles; they energize an artificial ecosystem of mechanical producers and consumers. What is important to recognize is that this acquisition is not only something applied by people from outside the natural order, a biotic innovation that ecosystems had to accommodate, but that it also replaces processes that humanity has practiced throughout its tenure on earth.

Industrial combustion is more than a new fire: it forces a reconstitution of that symbiotic relationship between people and planet that anthropogenic fire has mediated. Its effects cascaded wherever people lived, and then beyond, to wherever the output of humanity's new fire practices can penetrate, be they electricity from coal-fired dynamos carried hundreds of kilo-metres from their point of origin, or greenhouse gases loosed into the atmosphere. This is a new kind of fire ecology, for which the traditional descriptors of fire effects hardly apply.

The transformation – still unfolding after 200 years but instantaneous relative to biotic and geologic time – is the pyric equivalent of a bow shock or hydraulic jump. In short order, industrializing societies have restructured fire on their landscapes. In habitat after human habitat, the new fire has replaced the old. Flames and biofuelled burning have disappeared from homes, from factories, from cities and then from fields and forests. They have lingered longest in lightly used landscapes and protected natural areas such as parks and reserved woods, although even here societies charged with administering such areas have sought to abolish open fire, not only those set by people but by nature as well. This reformation might aptly be termed the pyric transi-tion after the well-known demographic transition that accom-panies industrialization. In both cases the immediate effect is a population explosion – in the one, of people; in the other, of fires – as old traditions persist and new practices appear. Then, over decades, the new replaces the old. Certainly something like this has characterized fire history. The shock of the transition begins with an overpopulation of fires, often abusive and promiscuous, and ends with the removal of open burning, so much so that the numbers plunge below replacement values. In this way, early industrializing societies experience a wave of destructive confla-grations, and fully industrialized ones undergo a fire famine as fire's abrupt removal shocks biota.

Industrial fire regimes

The mechanics of the transition are twofold. One level involves technological substitution; the other, outright suppression. The first occurs with industrial maturity and proceeds according to a logic of economic efficiency and legal requirements. The second depends also on a degree of sophistication in that active fire-fighting may require the apparatus of industrial fire in the form

Pump jack and bison, the new domain of patch burning: Tallgrass Prairie Preserve, Oklahoma.

of fire engines and pumps and electrically powered communication systems. The upshot is a much altered landscape mosaic underwritten by drastically different fire regimes.

The quick story: new combustion crowds out the old. Electric lights substitute for candles, gas stoves replace wood burners, diesel-guzzling tractors supplant oat-fuelled oxen. Instead of open flame restructuring woods there are chainsaws and wood chippers. Instead of fire liberating nutrients into soil, air and stream, fossil-fuelled factories break down fossil biomass to produce nitrogen, phosphorus and other fertilizers, while trucks haul them to distant sites and tractors sow them. Instead of temporarily fumigating a site using smoke and heat, or hoeing by selective fire, farmers spread artificial pesticides and herbicides and scarify with mechanical harrows drawn by tractors. Blueberry fields are 'burned' under propane jets drawn by tractors. Ethylene gas, without smoke, stimulates flowering. Free-burning fire disappears and closed combustion takes its place. A fossil fallow replaces the living.

When open fire does occur, its internal-combustion competitor quickly extinguishes it. In the past the best control was to

Fireplace: The Movie, 2003. Virtual fire: a video of fire to be shown on television, completing the metaphor of TV as an electronic hearth.

cultivate the landscape in such ways that it could not burn, or had built-in firewalls of incombustible barriers or fire-resistant plants, or was already deliberately burned. Such pre-emptive firing was a way to substitute controlled fire for wild fire. It had the advantage of keeping fire on the land. But as societies industrialize they tolerate less and less and will actively suppress flames wherever they occur. Unsurprisingly, they appeal to the machinery of internal combustion and other industrial inventions to pump water or chemicals, or to drop them from aircraft, or to transport crews by vehicles to fire flanks where they must run power tools. Pre-emptive burning and backfiring declines. The area burned shrinks. In built landscapes open fire can all but vanish; in wildlands it will shrivel until, interestingly, the trend may eventually reverse under considerations of cost, firefighter safety and ecological integrity.

What principles organize the landscapes of industrial fire? Many look similar because internal combustion tends to replace open burning much as silica replaces lignin in petrified wood. The realm of industrial combustion retains its lines of fire and fields of fire. Internal combustion runs on a matrix of roads (or flight paths) and burns within the patches – the factories, the power plants – of the built landscape. These are the energy pathways that carry and organize nutrients and species for an industrial ecology. They connect primary producers to consumers, they pump water for irrigation, they distribute the derived fertilizers and fumigants. They sustain the agents – people – that run this top-down ecosystem. Remove that combustion source and the system will collapse.

Most pre-industrial landscapes are agricultural; that is, they are shaped by anthropogenic fire in the service of farming and herding. The pyric transition has rebuilt such environments. No longer do farmers need to cultivate a fuel through fallowing in order to power draft animals, fertilize fields or kill noxious weeds and pests. They can run tractors, reapers and tillers on gasoline and diesel; they can lavish nitrogenous fertilizers on fields; they can spray herbicides and pesticides at will, typically from tractors, pumps or aircraft. Those chemicals derive largely from fossil biomass distilled through processes of industrial combustion. As H. T. Odum famously remarked, today a potato consists partly of petroleum. Moreover, what crops are grown (and when) depends on transport, which feeds on more petroleum. The entire economy of agricultural production has morphed from open flame to internal combustion, and from living fallow to fossil fallow.

These are only the obvious, first-order consequences. In reality the new combustion, like a boulder over a cliff, has set into motion a cascade of second- and third-order effects. Ecological services shrink; ecological goods such as biodiversity retreat to fence lines, right-of-ways and parks. As a cameo of such changes consider draft animals, which have become, like flame, largely ceremonial. The role of the Budweiser Clydesdales, for example, serves as a biotic equivalent of a celebratory bonfire.

After the pyric transition, a fire mosaic still exists but it is often no longer visible. Much as modern buildings are shaped by the threat of fire but rarely experience fire, so modern landscapes result from the application of anthropogenic fire, but it is a combustion rarely expressed as flame. It occurs internally or invisibly – distilled into petroleum fuels or sublimated into electricity. Of course not all modern energy derives from fire any more than all organic decomposition depends on burning, but most does, and almost all modern transport, which structures the flows of energy

Fire machined: the Corliss Engine at the American Centennial, in *Illustrated History of the Centennial Exposition, 1876* (New York, 1877). When he later saw a version at the Paris Exposition in 1990, Henry Adams wrote a meditation on the comparative power of the dynamo for the modern world against than of the Virgin for the medieval.

and goods, burns fossil biomass. Industrial fire ecology has its regimes and mosaics. It just doesn't show it openly.

There is one grand exception: the nature reserve, which industrial societies like to establish. In a sense these are the fallow fields of modern economies, and like the fallowed lands of old they hold most of the resident biodiversity. Not all such sites are naturally fire-prone, but if they can burn, they need to. Moreover, not all of those reserves are natural. Many are cultural landscapes, for which anthropogenic fire is a vital catalyst. In either case, removing fire may be ecologically disruptive, even catastrophic. If fire has been present for a long time it may have to remain in order to maintain a site's ecological integrity. Paradoxically, even as industrializing societies strive to eliminate open fire generally, they may have to retain or restore it on nature reserves.

This much is easily observed. The pyric transition, however, has not been systematically studied despite its significance as the entry into the modern world and the prime catalyst for global change. How any particular society manages the transition will vary by environment, history and cultural peculiarities. By linking hinterlands to urban markets it will stimulate burning in tropical landscapes through the conversion of woods to pastures, but the same process will dampen fire in arid landscapes

USGS map of large fires
in America, 1980–2005,
which is largely a map
of public lands.

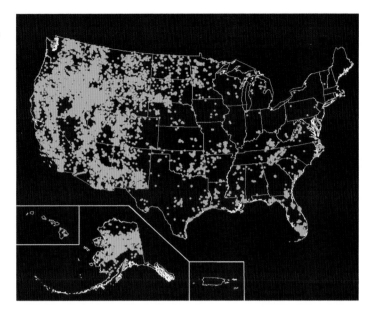

because overgrazing – a likely outcome – will strip away fine fuels. Countries that have a legacy of colonial fire management may well retain institutions and ideas from that era that will affect how they manage fire. They will typically have forest reserves, and forestry bureaus to administer them. They will often sponsor fire research, a topic not often found in places outside that imperial network. And of course there will be cultural differences. Canadians and Americans, for instance, despite having enormous similarities, manage wildland fire in distinctive ways, which derive from their divergent political structures and differing sense of national identity.

Such considerations may seem far removed from an ecology of fire. But the pyric transition creates an ecology that operates on different principles from the past. Previously, people had to interact with their natural environment; each could check or amplify the other. Wild fire had its own reality quite apart from anything people might do. Remove people, and fires would re-arrange themselves but could flourish regardless, much as wild sheep can thrive if domesticated sheep disappear. Industrial fire, however, cannot exist without people. Remove them and combustion ceases. Industrial fire is like an invented species that operates on the same chemistry as natural ones but is designed and nurtured in a lab. With fossil fuel combustion people have moved beyond domesticating nature's fires and have begun to invent new breeds from first principles. Since such fires exist only through people, how humanity sees the world and how people organize themselves through institutions will have enormous consequences for how fire actually appears on earth.

Enlightenment and empire

Two other events in particular have helped shape humanity's relationship to fire over the past 250 years. One is the emergence in Europe of modern science as a working doctrine; the other was a revival of European expansionism. Together they affected how fire came to be understood and used and how that perception propagated throughout the world.

Science proposed a novel way of deciphering nature. A new logic of discovery, experimentation and reasoning – mathematics – merged into a better way to read the book of nature and thus leave the arcane texts of the ancients behind. Reason challenged revelation. It could do what scholasticism and scripture could not: illuminate the darkness and sweep away ignorance and superstition. By the end of the seventeenth century a style of inquiry about nature was leaving the study to spread throughout the culture in what was self-consciously referred to as Enlightenment. Discipline after discipline found itself disrupted and remade, not unlike businesses in recent times unbundling and reorganizing under the blows of the digital revolution and Internet.

The impact on fire generally fell into two categories. In one, science gradually bonded with engineering, or mechanical tinkering, to speed up innovation and improve the new fire engines. The major inventions – not least, the steam engine itself – did not evolve out of Galileo's work on gravity and the 'mechanics' of the planets, or Newton's *Principia* (1687). They did not emerge from the lab but from incremental advances with prior inventions. The breakthrough work had nothing to do with natural philosophy, as it was known, except that both exhibited an enthusiasm for applied reasoning. The first major scientific works on the topic, like Sadi Carnot's, pondered existing steam engines. They studied the inventions as they would rivers or comets in order to bring them under the new regime of Reason. Eventually, however, a fast-maturing science helped sharpen and quicken the tempo of tinkering. Like an atlatl fixed to a spear, science added intellectual leverage.

The second impact was to challenge traditional knowledge. What did not derive from scientific methods was not verified and was hence considered a lesser form of knowing. However incomplete, scientific inquiry was deemed superior to any other forms, which were deemed suspect if not openly scorned. Agronomists dismissed as intrinsically 'primitive' any species of farming or grazing that relied on burning. An Enlightened agricultural revolution required that alternatives to fire be promoted.

The upshot was to dismiss tens of millennia of humanity's practical wisdom regarding fire and its usage. The new mode of thinking acted like intellectual acid, dissolving the grout of erstwhile understanding. Society split between educated elites and practitioners, the former suspicious of fire and the latter committed to its usage. The new knowledge was robust in the built environment and its mechanical menagerie but was dismally inadequate in field and forest.

All this might not have mattered had the Enlightenment and its peculiar pyrophobia remained in temperate Europe, which is among the least fire-prone places on earth. But they did not. The Anthropocene coincided with a revived expansion of Europe, what is recognized generally as the classic age of imperialism. Empires, whether of trade or settlement (or science), were vehicles for disseminating industrial fire, a fire science, and institutions for governing how fire should exist on the land.

That task fell to, or rather was seized by, foresters. Even though most fire existed within the matrix of agriculture, forestry declared itself the oracle and engineering corps for fire. Its values would dominate. With its roots in academic silviculture, forestry already claimed scientific authority. With its organization into a guild, it had a collective identity, internal cohesion and intellectual discipline that transcended particular national or imperial bounds. With control over forest reserves, a centrepiece in state-sponsored conservation, foresters acquired political power. With political power came intellectual control over the agenda of fire research and over fire practices generally.

All this converged on an extraordinary global project: the establishment of extensive public forests and parks primarily in British, French and Dutch colonies, and in settler societies such as America, Australia, Canada and the more complex South Africa. What foresters everywhere shared was a fear and hatred of fire, and a determination to remove it so far as possible. Scratch a forester, an old saying goes, and you'll find a firefighter. In fact, many forestry authorities such as Bernhard Fernow did not accept fire protection as a discipline within forestry. Rather, it was a precondition for forestry. Until the landscape was secure from flames, forestry could not perform its promised marvels.

Albert Bierstadt, *White Mountains, New Hampshire, c.* 1865, oil on paper. Rapid colonization meant that even areas like the northeastern u.s. that lacked a natural basis for fire burned violently. Fire control was a way to discipline settlement and lessen the wastage of woods.

Fernow is himself a marvellous example of how forestry followed empire. Trained as a state forester in Prussia, he married an American woman and moved to the u.s., where he became America's first professional forester. From 1886 to 1898 he ran a small government agency, the Bureau of Forestry, lodged in the Department of Agriculture, that also advised the national government on how to manage the forest reserves it began creating in 1891. He then established the nation's first forestry school at Cornell, until controversy shut it down. Undeterred, he moved north to the University of Toronto, where he again created a national forestry school, participated in conservation projects and advised practising foresters from Nova Scotia to the Canadian Rockies. His original training persisted as he carted views about fire learned in the regimented pine plantations of Prussia around the world like an axe. America's fire scene left him outraged and contemptuous. Until fires were controlled, nothing worthwhile could happen.

Those were attitudes typical of his forester cohort. Although they adapted formal precepts to particular circumstances, they typically railed against traditional fire usage and sought to abolish it wherever possible. Probably the most significant experiment occurred in British India in the latter nineteenth century. The effort failed, not only because it was too vast and understaffed an undertaking, but because its conception was fundamentally flawed. It belonged with an engineering age that sought to dam and straighten out streams to improve watersheds and to pump up game herds by exterminating predators. There was little appreciation that fire might have a beneficent ecological role or that, conversely, removing it might unhinge whole biota. Fire protection was part of a progressive view of the world that suffused many castes. When Rudyard Kipling wrote a story that explained what Mowgli did after he grew up, he made him a forest guard for the Indian Forest Department where one of his primary tasks is to guard against jungle fires.

As the decades rolled by, the pernicious consequences of fire exclusion became more apparent. The ecological health of wildlands suffered; feral fires replaced tamed ones; outbreaks became

Mariposa Grove of Big Trees in Yosemite National Park, as they appeared in 1890.

Mariposa Grove in 1960, now so overgrown as a result of fire's exclusion that you can hardly see the trees for the forest, all of which is at serious risk from catastrophic fire.

more savage. By the 1960s in the U.S., agencies that oversaw public lands sought to revise policy and practice to restore fire. Interestingly, this happened as state-sponsored forestry began to implode globally amid a wave of decolonization. Other agencies such as national parks and wildlife refuges challenged forestry for control over public lands. Other sciences, such as ecology and wildlife biology, questioned its claim to scientific surety. Cultural values urged that ecological goods and services replace the crude commodity production that forestry had boosted. The idea has spread generally that something like natural fire should reclaim places seeking to perpetuate something like natural conditions. Most managers of wilderness and parklands consider fire's suppression, not its presence, as the problem; a naturally ignited fire they regard as innocent until proven guilty. In many respects

Restoring fire to the sequoia groves.

forestry has been disgraced as an authority for the management of landscapes outside commercial woodlots and has reluctantly yielded its privileged standing.

The great divide: fires flaring, fires dying, fires revived

The pyric transition is the great divide in modern fire history, and because fire is so elemental to earth it serves as a kind of historic terminator that separates the planet into two dominions. There is day to one side, night to the other, and a blurred moving border between them.

Ahead, there is bright flame. All around them people saw flames. They saw them in their hearths, on their stoves, in their candles. They saw them seasonally in fields, paddocks and woods. They celebrated around bonfires. They worshipped with fire on the altar and beneath the icon. Their battlefields burned like cities, their cities burned like forests, their forests burned with wildfires. They imagined fire as a theophany or a fundamental principle of natural philosophy.

Behind, fire faded. It ceased to be a general technology and a companionable presence amid human habitations. Partly, it disappeared through outright suppression: open flames were condemned, increasingly restricted, and where they appeared unwanted they were smothered. Mostly, though, modern society snuffed out fires through a process of technological substitution. Internal combustion, electric lights, gas furnaces and assorted dynamos and generators began to do what previously only open burning could, and, unlike fire's side-effects, their by-products are largely invisible or are exported into the future. The world lit by fire went dark, replaced by artificial illumination and virtual flame. Only in special sites, as though they were exhibits in a natural history museum, did fire endure, and in fact was preserved, as one might adjust the temperature and humidity of a sealed room to preserve a parchment exhumed from the past.

It is along that transition, however, that the two mix, benignly or violently, commanding the mind's eye. Here are the fires most violent, extravagant, brutal, telegenic, damaging and outrageous.

A satellite view of the interface. Burned public land and city, Los Padres National Forest and Santa Barbara, California, Jesusita fire, 13 May 2009.

These are the societies still burning yet stirring in industrial combustion, frontiers raw with land clearing or land abandonment; and they are the industrial societies pushing an exurban frontier over formerly rural lands and against reserved wildlands. Collectively they create the illusion that free-burning fire has slipped its leash and threatens everywhere. In truth, the grand story of fire on earth is of fire's recession, of its replacement by internal combustions. As the world burns, the terminator moves, and darkness washes away the flames. Still, the general loss of familiarity among developed nations can make the appearance of large burns, when they return, all the more vivid and threatening.

10 Megafire

Industrial combustion does not look like fire. Hidden in machines, its fuels stocked in tanks and bottles, moved by pumps and fed through hoses, its oxygen also refined and then channelled into combustion chambers, the burning itself contained within special sites, its effluents too distilled from smoke and removed by pipes and smokestacks far from the place of actual combustion – all this is fire engineered. It is culture's second nature of fire. What flame integrates, industrial burning reduces, refines and reassembles. The outcome bears little visible relation to fire in its vernacular sense. Indeed, the outcome is typically not visible at all.

But if the process doesn't look much like fire, its consequences do. By transmuting fossil fuel into firepower, industrial combustion has remade the setting that free-burning fire synthesizes. Its gaseous emissions are unhinging the climate in ways that promote planetary warming. Its fire engines allow for a massive restructuring of transportation, and hence of markets, which redefines the uses of land. It allows formerly impenetrable places like rainforests to be cleared and converted to other purposes. It makes other places, perhaps long inhabited farmlands, less valuable and so leads to their abandonment, with fire as an aftershock. It can cause yet other sites, now valued by urban populations for their natural qualities, to become special reserves, with a corresponding shift in their regimen of fire. It makes fire protection powerful by granting it mechanical muscle, and it can cause control to collapse if those fire engines can no longer work.

Trees torching as a fire moves from the surface to the canopy. Magnify this escalation in intensity over thousands of hectares and you have a formula for megafire.

As countries enter the pyric transition they experience a riot of promiscuous and often abusive burning. Once the transition is established, however, those flames quiet and, in the eyes of their resident societies, seem to disappear. Fire slides into a smoky and benighted past, along with serfdom or smallpox. Then, if the lands are intrinsically fire-prone, or if climatic changes, introduced weeds or human migration make them so, fire returns to places made newly vulnerable. Like free-burning fire, the process at a planetary scale is patchy. An earth that appeared to be moving from a condition of routine flame to its mechanical sequestering or outright extinction has experienced an apparent rekindling. Like an ancient plague thought vanquished, fire has returned. Earth has entered its Age of Megafires.

The term 'megafire' was invented to describe the small fraction of wildland fires in America that, during the onset of the twenty-first century, had become very large. But the expression is elastic and can easily embrace a range of large-scale planetary burnings. If the sublimation of open fire into machines is the dominant trend of planetary combustion, its dark doppelganger is the megafire. Consider the following menagerie of megafires as a sample of the contemporary state of earthly burning.

Making new lands

Begin with new lands. This is an industrial-strength revival of an old practice by which societies shift 'wild' or subsistence lands into a more modern economy. Its boldest expressions today are in the tropics, most spectacularly in Amazonia and Borneo; in the post-Second World War era it could be found in the Soviet Union's 'virgin lands' scheme, in Australia's determination to develop its tropical north, Canada's economic colonization of its boreal hinterlands, especially the Northwest Territories, and in America's industrial settlement of Alaska, then newly admitted as a state. Note that all these regions are less-developed portions of large countries resolved to modernize their territorial estate. Behind those frontiers lie the historic experiences of widespread settlement in North America and Australasia, and behind that the medieval and earlier colonization of Europe, China, India and older civilizations either overlooked or overwhelmed by subsequent migrations.

What distinguishes the modern expressions of new land creation are their ties to industrialization, their suddenness, and their penetration into regions not previously subject to whole-sale conversion. Without ties to export markets made possible by fossil-fuel-powered transport, it is hard to imagine the abrupt movement of peoples and the ability to translate rainforest into marketable commodities on a subcontinental scale. Research continues to suggest that Amazonia, prior to the Portuguese conquest, had a serious human population that had transformed those places into sophisticated agricultural landscapes, and that the subsequent patterns characterized by swiddeners and hunter-foragers are the shattered remnants of once flourishing societies. But disease and slaving had decimated those populations, rain-forest reclaimed those sites, and the modern era has started the process over again.

The reasons behind the transformations are several. One is economic: a market for meat, soy or palm oil can nominally support a place once its forests have been strip-mined off. Another is social: the desire to move people from what the state perceives as overpopulated regions to underpopulated ones. 'The people without lands to the lands without people'. State-sponsored transmigration schemes have sought to relocate landless peoples from Brazil's northeast to its interior, and from teeming Java to seemingly vacant Kalimantan. And behind them, helping to rally the state, is a geopolitical concern: the fear that places remote from administrative control, that are not tightly integrated into a national apparatus, may be vulnerable to attacks, insurgencies or secession. The migration, however, would be unlikely to happen – certainly not on the scale and rapidity observed – without an economy and a technology based on internal combustion.

The thumbnail stories run in parallel. For Brazil the military government during the 1960s decided to develop Amazonia. Rude roads were followed by land clearing. What was slashed was then burned. The land was re-burned annually to refresh it, mostly for low-productivity pastures. The basin filled with smoke, the planetary atmosphere got a heavy dose of greenhouse gases, and a world increasingly concerned about biodiversity, climate change and indigenous peoples took alarm. Burning Brazil became an emblem of a coming environmental apocalypse. For Indonesia, another dictatorship elected likewise to develop its outlying islands, particularly Borneo. A similar scenario followed in which roads opened new lands which then fell to chainsaws and bulldozers; some was converted into farms for relocated peasants while the largest sites were transformed into plantations for palm oil. In place of Brazil's fabled forests, dense with leafy carbon, Borneo had thick peatlands, even more heavily laden with stored carbon. Drained and burned, these seasonally immersed the wider region in smoke. Because of this, by the onset of the twenty-first century Indonesia was the fourth largest producer of greenhouse gases on earth.

While both conversions have created fire problems, they do not have fire solutions, for fire and smoke are by-products of larger social movements. They are symptoms rather than sources; they are not the media-grabbing megafires of soaring conflagrations but a more insidious pathology of extensive, planned burning; and their violence is measured in ecological damage rather than in the length or longevity of their flames. Some ameliorative measures are possible, but it is difficult to swat out blazes across landscapes the size of France. This is less a contagion that spreads from one point outward, like a cholera epidemic from a faulty spigot, than a mass flowering of weeds when conditions are suitable. To remedy the consequences by addressing the fires alone is to mis-define the problem and will likely result in misallocated attention and actions. It may, for example, lead to political theatre in which air tankers and suppression crews attack the fires even as the burning continually reignites because the fires serve the interests of political and economic elites. Lop off the top of the weed, and it resprouts from the root.

Leaving old lands

Such are the megafires of fast-industrializing frontier societies with large hinterlands. The obverse is late-industrializing societies with long-settled landscapes like those along the northern littoral of the Mediterranean. Move a bit west to include Portugal and Galicia and you have some of the most fire-scarred places on earth.

These are agricultural countrysides that assumed their fundamental shapes before Roman times. Their geography favours fire: Mediterranean landscapes are heavily salted with tough pyrophytes. The lands have been burned by people for millennia. But they have known fire within the constraints of close cultivation or the parameters of pastoral economies. Fire was cropped, hoed, chewed, trampled, pruned, planted and herded, or even folded, as it were, into the flock. These were anthropogenic fires on anthropogenic landscapes. Occasionally they would go feral during plagues, wars, droughts or other outbreaks of social unrest when, for a while, the land could no longer be tended in ways that tamed fire. But fire control returned with the return of a social order.

The outbreaks of the past few decades are different. In particular those in Greece, Spain and Portugal – all emerged from dictatorships, entered the European Union and the global market and began a rapid industrialization. The most striking expression of this transition was the spontaneous migration from country-side to city, from small farms and flocks to Athens, Thessaloniki, Lisbon, Oporto, Barcelona and Madrid. More and more of the countryside was left to the old and the young. In Iberia the process of depopulation had begun earlier, with efforts to replace low-value pasturage with plantation forests; now it was simply abandoned to grow up with rough scrub. Traditional fires escaped and mingled with a residue of incendiarism, a pattern of politi-cal arson aimed at dispossessing plantations (often of despised exotics like eucalypts). The old ways of containing fire broke down. Large swathes of land burned.

It was a new firescape, prone to eruptive burning, and if only as a matter of public safety and as a political necessity to be seen to be doing something, officials responded by assuming the appa-ratus of states with mature fire protection. They brought in air tankers and helicopters. They created mobile fire crews. They fought the flames as the major firepowers did, and they began taking the kind of casualties those nations did. There was a ten-dency, too, towards remaking firefighting agencies into all-hazard emergency response institutions. This went furthest in Greece, which removed rural fire protection from its Forest Service and handed it to an urban-based firefighting ministry. When com-bined with landscapes in turmoil, the result has been disaster. Fires synthesize their surroundings. Identify that setting, and you identify the character of fire. Control that setting, and you control fire. Societies lost control over the countryside, which meant they lost control over fire. The devouring flames needed fighting, but no less than in Brazil or Borneo, agencies would be merely hotspotting unless they could get to grips with the unravelling landscape.

Fire management intertwines with land use like vines on a trellis – that is the final message. The Mediterranean fire scene offered a weird inversion of the tropical one. The one displayed a pushy frontier, actively converting fire-immune woods into com-bustibles, while the other, a retiring frontier, left a revanchist fire-boosting biota in its wake. They faced each other like images

overleaf: New lurid light on a source of ancient illumination: the Parthenon flanked with wildfire, 23 August 2009.

passing through a looking glass. For neither was fire control alone an adequate response.

Losing control

Yet there are places where the disintegration of fire protection institutions does explain the resurgence of large fires. The best examples hark back to the break-up of the Soviet Union and its political satellites. Wildland firefighting can be expensive, especially when it relies on airpower. If a state collapses, it may find those costs too great, and without the capacity to knock down fires at their onset, the burns may metastasize into megafires.

The Soviet Union fell apart in 1991. It bequeathed an extensive fire protection apparatus to its offspring, one committed to both ground and aerial forces. The USSR had some 8,500 smoke-jumpers, cross-trained for heli-rappelling, most of them based east of the Urals. A major escalation of the apparatus had followed stubborn, widespread fires around Moscow and European Russia in 1972. The Russian Federation inherited the bulk of those forces; and then another bout of serious fires around Moscow in 1992 prevented a sudden implosion. But gradually capacity eroded, capabilities deteriorated, and the full measure of diminution was disguised by shrinking the amount of land under formal protection.

Burning, typically outbursts on a roughly decadal (or double-decadal) cycle, is routine in the boreal biota, and where people farm or log, they add fires during the spring and autumn. The new regime began in the perestroika era. In May 1987 perhaps 12–14 million ha (30–35 million ac) burned in Transbaikalia; the system was locally overwhelmed. So while the threat remained constant, and may have worsened under the impress of global warming, the ability to respond steadily deteriorated. In 2007 the situation sharply worsened when a new forest law transferred responsibility for fire protection from the state to companies granted logging concessions. The predictable outcome was a further loss in capacity as companies pulled back their investments in fire control. Particularly in boreal landscapes, fire protection

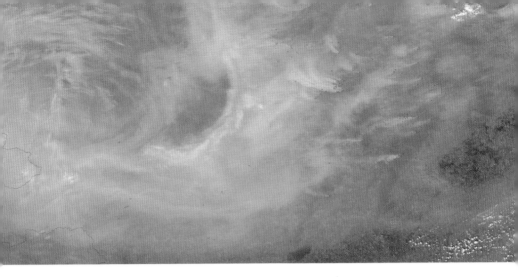

Visible from space: Moscow immersed in smoke, 7 August 2010.

is a calculated gamble because it requires large fixed costs, but big fires come episodically. Across northern Eurasia some place would always burn, although most years most places would escape.

But 2010 was not most years. Big fires rippled through Siberia. The worst outbreak occurred in the Volga region, which endured a tenacious drought that drew fires as carrion does scavengers. The apparatus was unable to cope. Probably under the best of circumstances it would have bent, if not broken; the fires moved more or less unchecked save for sporadic rural resistance. This fire season became notorious, however, not because of the damages inflicted through the rural countryside or across the looming taiga, but because it smoked in Moscow. It became a fixture of the global media as Muscovites and tourists, wearing surgical masks, staggered across a Red Square under a sky reddened with soot and smoke like a dry fog. This smoke did not actually emanate from the marauding megafires but from nearby peatlands. Small fires, much smoke, major publicity.

The region suffered through record heat; probably any aspect of the surrounding landscape would have been readied to burn. But the peatlands fuel had a history of being drained and partly mined; that heritage expanded the range and depth of combustibles. Probably the community could have coped with one of those three factors – weather, land use history or lost fire control; it might even have muddled through two of them; but it could not cope with three. The only way to suppress the smoke was to flood the smouldering peat, an exercise in reverse engineering, and to restore a bolder agency to muster firefighting capabilities equivalent to the environmental challenge.

At least Moscow's full-immersion baptism in smoke gave some prominence to the Russian catastrophe. There was no media interest in the far worse disaster that had been unfolding in Mongolia. When it was a Soviet satellite, Mongolia had an enforced (if unwelcome) social order and a wildland firefighting capability modelled on that across the border. Before its independence, Mongolia had more smokejumpers than the United States. Then, overnight, it crumbled into Gobi dust.[1]

All national institutions seemed to fold. The collapse of the economy sent many urbanites back to the steppes, if only in the spring to search for red deer antlers (for the Chinese market). But springtime offers the prime conditions for major fires as the winds blow, the snow is gone, and the grasses and larch understories have not yet greened up. Many of the dispersed people kindled fires for cooking and warmth, a fraction of which bolted free; and some set fires to burn off the dry, obscuring grasses to expose marketable antlers. Meanwhile nature echoed the worsening social conditions with repeated droughts. In 1996 and 1997 some 10.7 million ha and 12–14 million ha respectively burned, roughly eighteen times the previous annual average. A horde of fires thundered across the landscape.

Carved out of central Eurasia – a continental climate given to recurrent drought and dry spells, framed between the boreal taiga and the Gobi Desert, a society artificially parsed into urban and pastoral, a social order pummelled by sudden economic and political change – Mongolia was always a good bet to suffer when those precariously balanced parts came unglued. The country itself was a construct. It had held its fires in check through tight state control over society and state-sponsored fire suppression. When one part of this yurt of grass blew down, it took the others with it.

The upshot is that while Mongolia has a hideous fire problem, few options exist within the fire community to ameliorate it. It cannot stop drought or replace steppes with incombustibles.

It cannot reconstitute Mongolian society and economy. It cannot even chase fires with the instruments of internal combustion. Until Mongolia can refashion itself in ways that place fire control under the discipline of vernacular society, fire management may itself become as migratory as its peoples.

Loosening control

What has astonished most, perhaps, is the return of big fires to countries like America and Australia which are fully industrialized and had, it seemed, fashioned durable mechanisms for fire control. Only two to three fires out of every hundred escaped initial attack, and only two or three of those blew up into monsters, but that tiny fraction (0.1 per cent) accounted for 95 per cent or more of the burned area and over 85 per cent of costs. These were the fires that first received the sobriquet 'megafires'. They seemed to signify the terrifying prospect by which giant, deadly burns, once scrubbed out of the landscape, were returning, like the reappearance of a mutant strain of polio. The term itself commanded media attention. The global warming crowd in particular seized on megafire smoke plumes as hard evidence of climate's threat.[2]

Once again, however, the reality was more complex, though not so complex that it was beyond understanding or corrective measures. Big fires do not result from any single factor but from several that compound in particular ways. With mega-wildfires those factors belonged in social realms as well as environmental. In the u.s. they also pivoted around a great paradox: the public agencies had set a goal of increasing the amount of burning on lands under their jurisdiction. They got it.

The dramatic reduction in burned area over the preceding decades had been purchased with borrowed time. Climate had been benign, firefighting had mechanized rapidly, and fires could be easily removed from landscapes that experienced frequent surface fires such that a small investment of effort yielded large returns. But combustibles continued to grow and thicken as woods invaded prairie and young trees packed forests with needles from ground to canopy. Difficult fires became more difficult still, as agencies fought the curve of diminishing returns. Costs rose, not least the cost in firefighter casualties. And fires removed were fires that no longer did the biological work a landscape might need. An ecological deficit swelled to match its financial one. By the 1970s the agencies that oversaw America's public lands determined to restore fire to something like its historic vigour.

By now the climate was turning in ways that favoured drought and longer seasons for burning, and bad seasons crowded together. Landscapes were filled with accessible fuels: surfaces were layered with windfall and scrub, patchy canopies had closed, the dappled texture that had helped break and buffer fire's intensity and spread had often smeared into a medium ideal for carrying big fires. The legacy of past practices and the prognosis of future climates primed many landscapes for a breakout of wholesale burning.

The environment, however, was only one side of fire's new triangle because land use and fire programmes also realigned in ways that favoured megafires. Significant fractions of public land went into wilderness or parks that favoured free-burning flame, and once-rural lands outside the public land boundaries filled with exurban settlements. The one argued against aggressive fire suppression, the other, for its augmentation. Both, moreover, found it difficult to justify putting firefighters at risk. The wild didn't need firefighting in the classic way; the exurban didn't warrant putting firefighters in harm's way for a built landscape that was often inherently indefensible; tricky fires were best attacked indirectly with lots of backfiring and multiple fires were better handled as one complex rather than many. The emerging consensus encouraged agencies to back off.

In brief, agencies sought to redirect an existing apparatus in ways that would tolerate or actively promote more burned land. Climate, land use, fire practices – all pushed in the same direction. More land burned. Some big fires became monsters. 'Megafire' joined 'road rage' as a metaphoric signpost of contemporary times. The expression, if not the reality, migrated from America to cognate fire countries.

Missing fires

Yet despite costly and sometimes fatal wildfires, fire agencies in developed countries obsessed less over their megafires than over their missing fires. After the pyric transition the population of fires, like that of people, failed to reach replacement values, which is to say, there were too few fires to sustain the desired firescapes. In the judgement of most fire officers, there were not enough fires of the right sort to do the ecological work required. The impending crisis was not simply of wildfires mutating into megafires but of benign fires gone missing. An outside observer might well ponder the paradox by which fire agencies descried the rising tide of burned area while simultaneously pleading for more fire. A simple resolution would hold that they had too much of the wrong kind of fire and too little of the right. But behind that observation lay another. The earth had too little fire and too much combustion.

Epilogue: Two Fire Worlds

Today, across the earth, three fires – natural, anthropogenic, industrial – are sorting themselves into two grand realms of combustion. At global and regional scales, the divide appears as the pyric transition. The border can be sharp. The two Koreas, for example, share a common environment and ethnicity, and save for the past 60 years, a common heritage, yet the Demilitarized Zone that divided the peninsula half a century ago also split their fire history. South Korea made the pyric transition, North Korea did not. Evening satellite photos of lights, largely electrical, show the South aglow with urban patches, while the North is conspicuous in its dark absence. MODIS satellite images of open burning invert that picture. The North is speckled with fires, many along the border, while the South has scattered and exceptional fires.

That same process of partitioning characterizes the planet. Europe and Africa, for example, show a similar splitting. In this case there are significant environmental, cultural and historical differences since Sub-Saharan Africa can support free-burning fire in ways that temperate Europe cannot. Yet there are portions of Mediterranean Europe where the pyric transition has not yet worked through to completion and these overflow with wildfires, and there are places in Africa – notably South Africa – where industrial combustion has progressed to the point that open burning is fast fading. The scene reinforces, too, the role people play in sorting out the two realms. They not only tend industrial combustion but determine how it interacts with other forms of

MODIS Europe and Africa. DMSP nighttime lights processed by the NOAA National Geophysical Data Center.

fire. Some African countries with massive fossil fuel resources lack the institutions to transfer that firepower to ordinary life and landscapes. Offshore rigs flare off natural gas with a brightness like supernovas, while interior landscapes ripple with surface fires. Some northern European countries struggle to reintroduce fire for ecological benefits to lands set apart for nature protection.

The actual dynamics of pyric sorting are a kind of three-body problem for which there is no precise solution. Lightning will kindle whatever is available wherever possible. Industrial combustion will occur wherever people want it. What is getting lost is that intermediate realm of anthropogenic fire. Developed nations have plenty of fossil biomass burning and, where dry lightning and nature reserves are prominent, an abundance of natural fires. While some regions have retained a tradition of deliberate burning amid this scene, it is rare and attributable only to the persistence of cultural traditions. Mostly the world is fissioning into one realm or the other, a setting in which lightning and anthropogenic fire coexist and compete, or one in which lightning and industrial combustion do. What is fading is the middle world that humanity has occupied for nearly all its evolutionary existence, the world in which people have served as brokers for fire's ecological presence.

Earth remains a fire planet. How fire appears, what biological role it assumes, what technological work it does – all will depend on how humanity sees itself as a fire creature and fire

Frederic Edwin Church, *Christian on the Borders of the Valley of the Shadow of Death*, 1847, oil on canvas. Humanity entering a new world of fire.

monopolist, how it understands its place in the great scheme of things and how it seeks to reconcile the Faustian bargain it made long ago that brought us power and made us responsible for fire's application and absence. Fire wild, fire tame, fire mechanized – the torch remains in our hands, subject to the whims and wishes of our heads and hearts as we seek to divide three into two and have something left over.

REFERENCES

3 Fire Creature

1 My analysis follows closely R. W. Wrangham and N. L. Conklin-Brittain, 'The Biological Significance of Cooking in Human Evolution', *Comparative Biochemistry and Physiology, Part A*, 136 (2003), pp. 35–46. These ideas have been elaborated (though not enhanced) in Richard Wrangham, *Catching Fire: How Cooking Made Us Human* (New York, 2009), see esp. pp. 55–81.
2 Wrangham, *Catching Fire*, p. 18, quoting a study in Germany. On myths, see Sir James Frazer, *Myths on the Origin of Fire* (London, 1930; reprinted New York, 1974).
3 Pliny the Elder and Vannoccio Biringuccio quoted in Cyril Stanley Smith and Martha Teach Gnudi, trans. and eds, *The Pirotechnia of Vannoccio Biringuccio* (Cambridge, MA, 1966; reprint), p. 336.
4 Quoted in Gaston Bachelard, *The Psychoanalysis of Fire*, trans. Alan C. M. Ross (Boston, MA, 1964), p. 60.
5 Lydia V. Pyne and Stephen J. Pyne, *The Last Lost World: Ice Ages, Human Origins, and the Invention of the Pleistocene* (New York, 2012). Specific quotations as follows: Carl Sauer, 'Fire and Early Man', in John Leighly, *Land and Life: A Selection from the Writings of Carl Ortwin Sauer* (Berkeley, CA, 1963), p. 295; Loren Eiseley, 'Man the Firemaker', in *The Star Thrower* (San Diego, CA, 1978), pp. 47, 49; Pierre Teilhard de Chardin, *The Phenomenon of Man* (New York, 1976), p. 160; Claude Lévi-Strauss, *The Raw and the Cooked: Mythologiques*, vol. 1 (New York, 1969), p. 164; Edmund Leach quoted in Wrangham, *Catching Fire*, p. 12.

4 Fire Works: Anthropogenic Fire Practices

1 T. H. Mitchell, *Journal of an Expedition into the Interior of Tropical Australia* (London, 1848), p. 306.

2 H. H. Finlayson, *The Red Centre* (Sydney, 1946), pp. 64–7.
3 Aldo Leopold, *Game Management* (New York, 1933), p. xxxi.

5 **Famous Fires: An Anthology**

1 Wallace Stegner, 'A Sense of Place', in *Where the Bluebird Sings to the Lemonade Springs* (New York, 2002), p. 205.
2 The full story of the fire along with citations is told in Stephen J. Pyne, *Awful Splendour: A Fire History of Canada* (Vancouver, 2007), pp. 61–3.
3 Harrison Salisbury, *The Great Black Dragon Fire: A Chinese Inferno* (Boston, MA, 1989), pp. 159–60.
4 Reported in A. S. Jackson, 'Wildfire in the Great Plains Grasslands', *Proceedings Fourth Annual Tall Timbers Fire Ecology Conference, March 18–19, 1965* (Tallahassee, FL, 1965), p. 245.
5 Published ten years later: V. B. Shostakovitch, 'Forest Conflagrations in Siberia', *Journal of Forestry*, XXIII/4 (1925), pp. 365–71. On the 2010 Russian fire, see Johann G. Goldammer, 'Preliminary Assessment of the Fire Situation in Western Russia, 15 August 2010', published by the Global Fire Monitoring Center (Freiburg, 2010).
6 R. H. Luke and A. G. McArthur, *Bushfires in Australia* (Canberra, 1977), pp. 339–44.
7 For the best single summary of the 2002–3 fires, see S. Ellis, P. Kanowski and R. Whelan, *Report of the National Inquiry on Bushfire Mitigation and Management* (Council of Australian Governments, 2004). For a survey of the many inquiries, see P. J. Kanowski, R. J. Whelan and S. Ellis, 'Inquiries following the 2002–03 Australian bushfires: common themes and future directions for Australian bushfire mitigation and management', *Australian Forestry*, LXVIII/2 (2005), pp. 76–86.

6 **Fire Studied and Fire Made**

1 Gaston Bachelard, *The Psychoanalysis of Fire*, trans. Alan C. M. Ross (Boston, MA, 1987), p. 7.
2 Quoted in Cyril Smith and Martha Gnudi, *The Pirotechnia of Vannoccio Biringuccio* (Cambridge, MA, 1966), p. xxvii.
3 Figures from Bernard Teague, et al., *Final Report: Summary*, 2009 Victorian Bushfires Royal Commission (Melbourne, 2010), p. 15.

7 Fire Painted

1 George Catlin, *Letters and Notes* (Picadilly, London, 1841), vol. 2, p. 17.
2 Ibid.
3 See Stephen J. Pyne, 'Untamed Art', *Forest History Today* (Fall 2008), pp. 48–57. For a sample of the bogus claims made for reproductions, see the article and subsequent letters in *Life* (31 March 1941), p. 77; and (21 April 1941), p. 11. For an introduction to the Australian group see William Splatt, *The Heidelberg School: The Golden Summer of Australian Painting* (Ringwood, Victoria, 1989).
4 Madeleine Say, 'Black Thursday: William Strutt's "Itinerant Picture"', *The La Trobe Journal*, LXXV (Autumn 2005); Christine Downer, 'Bushfire Panic', in Daniel Thomas, ed., *Creating Australia: 200 Years of Art, 1788–1988* (Sydney, 1988), pp. 44–6; and Heather Curnow, *The Life and Art of William Strutt, 1825–1915* (Martinborough, 1980).

8 Fire Celebrated

1 Passage quoted from Stephen Pyne, 'Old Fire, New Fire', *ISLE*, 6, no. 2 (Summer 1999), pp. 186–7.
2 Sir James Frazer, *Myths on the Origin of Fire* (London, 1930; reprinted New York, 1974), pp. 203, 226.
3 Prometheus text taken with slight modifications from Stephen Pyne, *Vestal Fire: An Environmental History, Told through Fire, of Europe and Europe's Encounter with the World* (Seattle, 1997), pp. 60–61.
4 Quoted in Pyne, *Vestal Fire*, pp. 76–7
5 Quoted in Sir James Frazer, *Balder the Beautiful: The Fire Festivals of Europe and the Doctrine of the External Soul* (New York, 1923), vol. I, p. 202.
6 Lady Wilde, *Ancient Legends, Mystic Charms, and Superstitions of Ireland* (London, 1888), vol. II, pp. 113–14.
7 See www.burningman.com; accessed 27 October 2010.

10 Megafire

1 The best descriptions of the Mongolian fire scene are the reports cached by the Global Fire Monitoring Center, available at www.fire.uni-freiburg.de. See for example http://www.fire.uni-freiburg.de/iffn/country/mn/mn_11.htm.; accessed 7 July 2011; Bayartaa Nyamjav et al., 'The Forest Fire Situation in Mongolia', *International Forest Fire News 36* (January–July 2007), pp. 446–66.

2   See Jerry Williams, '1910 Fires: A Century Later Could it Happen
    Again?', paper presented at the Inland Empire Society of American
    Foresters Annual Meeting, Wallace, ID, 20–22 May 2010; and Jerry
    T. Williams and Albert Hyde, 'The Mega-Fire Phenomenon:
    Observations from a Coarse-Scale Assessment with Implications
    for Foresters, Land Managers, and Policy-Makers', paper presented
    at the Society of American Foresters National Convention, Orlando,
    FL, 2 October 2009; accessed at www.fsx.org/pdf/2010/1910%20fires.
    saf.pdf; accessed 20 June 2011.

SELECT BIBLIOGRAPHY

Abbott, Ian, and Neil Burrows, eds, *Fire in Ecosystems of South-west Western Australia: Impacts and Management* (Leiden, 2003)

Bond, William J., and Brian W. van Wilgen, *Fire and Plants* (London, 1996)

Bradstock, Ross A., Jann E. Williams and A. Malcolm Gill, eds, *Flammable Australia: The Fire Regimes and Biodiversity of a Continent* (Cambridge, 2002)

Cochrane, Mark A., *Tropical Fire Ecology: Climate Change, Land Use, and Ecosystem Dynamics* (Chichester, 2009)

Cowling, Richard, ed., *The Ecology of Fynbos: Nutrients, Fire and Diversity* (Cape Town, 1992)

DeBano, Leonard E., Daniel G. Neary and Peter F. Ffolliott, *Fire's Effects on Ecosystems* (New York, 1998)

Frazer, Sir James, *Myths on the Origin of Fire* (London, 1930)

Goldammer, Johann Georg, and Valentin V. Furyaev, eds, *Fire in Ecosystems of Boreal Eurasia* (Dordrecht, 1996)

Goudsblom, Johan, *Fire and Civilization* (New York, 1992)

Krell, Alan, *Fire in Art and the Social Imagination* (London, 2011)

Kull, Chistian A., *Isle of Fire: The Political Ecology of Landscape Burning in Madagascar* (Chicago, 2004)

Myers, Ronald L., *Living with Fire: Sustaining Ecosystems and Livelihoods through Integrated Fire Management* (Tallahassee, 2006)

The Nature Conservancy, *Fire, Ecosystems and People: A Preliminary Assessment of Fire as a Global Conservation Issue* (Tallahassee, 2004)

Pyne, Stephen J., *Burning Bush: A Fire History of Australia* (New York, 1991)

——, *Fire in America: A Cultural History of Wildland and Rural Fire* (Seattle, 1995)

——, *Vestal Fire: An Environmental History, Told through Fire, of Europe and Europe's Encounter with the World* (Seattle, 1997)

——, *Fire: A Brief History* (Seattle, 2001)
——, *Year of the Fires: The Story of the Great Fires of 1910* (New York, 2001)
——, *Awful Splendour: A Fire History of Canada* (Vancouver, 2007)
——, Patricia L. Andrews and Richard D. Laven, *Introduction to Wildland Fire*, 2nd edn (New York, 1996)
Schroeder, Mark J., and Charles C. Buck, *Fire Weather*, Agriculture Handbook no. 360, U.S. Forest Service (Washington DC, 1970)
Tall Timbers Research Station, *Proceedings: Fire Ecology Conferences*, I–XXIV (Tallahassee, 1962–2011)
United Nations Economic Commission for Europe and the Food and Agriculture Organization of the United Nations, *International Forest Fire News* (New York, 1979–)
United States Department of Agriculture, Forest Service, *Wildland Fire in Ecosystems*, Rainbow Series
——, *Volume I: Wildland Fire in Ecosystems: Effects of Fire on Fauna*, ed. J. K. Smith, Gen. Tech. Report RMRS–GTR–42–vol. 1 (Odgen, UT, 2000)
——, *Volume II: Wildland Fire in Ecosystems: Effects of Fire on Flora*, ed. J. K. Brown and J. K. Smith, Gen. Tech. Report RMRS–GTR–42–vol. 2 (Ogden, UT, 2000)
——, *Volume III: Wildland Fire in Ecosystems. Effects of Fire on Cultural Resources and Archaeology*, Gen. Tech. Report RMRS–GTR–42–vol. 3 (Ogden, UT, 2012)
——, *Volume IV: Wildland Fire in Ecosystems: Effects of Fire on Soil and Water*, D. G. Neary, K. C. Ryan and L. F. DeBano, Gen. Tech. Report RMRS–GTR–42–vol. 4 (Ogden, UT, 2005)
——, *Volume V: Wildland Fire in Ecosystems: Effects of Fire on Air*, D. V. Sandberg *et al.*, Gen. Tech. Report RMRS–GTR–42–vol. 5 (Ogden, UT, 2002)
——, *Volume VI: Wildland Fire in Ecosystems: Fire and Nonnative Invasive Plants*, Gen. Tech. Report RMRS–GTR–42–vol. 6 (Ogden, UT, 2008)
Whelan, Robert, *The Ecology of Fire* (Cambridge, 1995)
Wrangham, Richard, *Catching Fire: How Cooking Made Us Human* (New York, 2009)
Wright, Henry A., and Arthur W. Bailey, *Fire Ecology: United States and Southern Canada* (New York, 1982)

ASSOCIATIONS AND WEBSITES

Major professional organizations for researchers and practitioners

International Association of Wildland Fire
www.iawfonline.org

Association for Fire Ecology
fireecology.org

Sources for current and historic information

Global Fire Monitoring Center
www.fire.uni-freiburg.de

Fire History Data, NOAA Paleoclimatology
www.ncdc.noaa.gov/paleo/impd/paleofire.html

Sites of regional interest

Global Wildland Fire Network
www.fire.uni-freiburg.de/GlobalNetworks/globalNet.html

USA: National Interagency Fire Center
www.nifc.gov

Canada: Canadian Interagency Forest Fire Centre
www.ciffc.ca

Australia: Australasian Fire Authorities Council
www.afac.com.au

Europe: Fire Paradox
www.fireparadox.org

ACKNOWLEDGEMENTS

This slim text summarizes a lifetime of study and collaboration with many, many colleagues. Let me thank here those who assisted with special tidbits of information and illustrations. Foremost is the indefatigable Johann G. Goldammer, as always reliable, knowledgeable and good-humoured. Others deserving of thanks include Marty Alexander, Brian Stocks and Ray Lovett. On the publication side I'd like to thank Reaktion's Publisher, Michael Leaman, Susannah Jayes, picture researcher, and Robert Williams, editor, for their gentle prods and generous advice.

PHOTO ACKNOWLEDGEMENTS

The author and the publishers wish to thank the below sources of
illustrative material and/or permission to reproduce it

AKG Images: p. 149; M. E. Alexander: p. 108; Amon Carter Museum, Fort
Worth, Texas: p. 65; Art Gallery of Ballarat, Victoria: p. 136; Ashmolean
Museum, Oxford: p. 123; Ateneum Art Museum, Helsinki: p. 22;
Berkshire Museum, Pittsfield, Massachusetts: p. 116; Brooklyn Museum,
New York: p. 127; Bureau of Land Management, u.s. Department of the
Interior: p. 156 (bottom); CEIF: p. 106 (bottom left); Canadian Forest
Service: p. 28 (B. J. Stocks); © DACS 2012: p. 40; Delta Entertainment
Corp.: p. 162; Department of Sustainability and Environment, Victoria:
p. 87; Derby Museum and Art Gallery: p. 105; Earth Observing Satellite,
NASA Earth Observatory: p. 173; Fire Museum, Yekaterinberg, Russia:
p. 130 (centre); Getty Images: pp. 180–89; J. G. Goldammer: pp. 36, 66,
67, 107; Hermitage Museum, St Petersburg: pp. 145, 152; Harry Hooper:
pp. 92–3; Library of Congress, Washington, DC: pp. 94 (Arnold Genthe),
156 (top); Ray Lovett: p. 21; Metropolitan Museum of Art, New York:
p. 102; Mildred Lane Kemper Art Museum, Washington University,
St Louis, Missouri: p. 16; Mitchell Library, Sydney: pp. 45 (Banks Papers),
54; Michigan Department of Natural Resources: p. 81; Musée des
Beaux-Arts André Malraux, Le Havre: p. 91; NASA: p. 183 (Global Fire
Monitoring Center); National Board of Antiquities, Finnish National
Museum: p. 70 (I. K. Inha); National Collection of Fine Arts, Smithsonian
Institution, Washington, DC: p. 126; National Gallery of Victoria,
Melbourne: p. 132; National Library of Australia, Canberra: pp. 54, 58;
National Park Service, u.s. Department of the Interior, Washington, DC:
pp. 31 (top), 90, 170 (top; George Reichel), 170 (bottom; Dan Taylor),
171 (Ted Young); National Oceanic & Atmospheric Administration:
p. 189 (courtesy Chris Elvidge); Olana State Historic Site, New York
State Office of Parks, Recreation, & Historic Preservation: p. 190; Paul:
p. 78; Stephen J. Pyne: pp. 6, 8, 20, 32, 43, 44, 51, 161; Press Association

INDEX